and then there was One

A Comprehensive Workbook Guide
for End-of-Life Preparedness and
Transitioning After the Loss of a Loved One

CHARLOTTE FOX

…because time and unforeseen occurrence befall them all.
—*Ecclesiastes 9:11*

and then there was one

A Comprehensive Workbook Guide for End-of-Life Preparedness and Transitioning After the Loss of a Loved One

Charlotte Fox, Author, Editor

Leighton H. Rockafellow
Attorney at Law
Contributing Editor

3rd Edition
Copyright 2013 © Charlotte Fox
ISBN 9780961746834
Revised May 2015
Nation of Publication: United States

(Previous Second Edition: ISBN 9780961746872)

FOX PUBLICATIONS, LLC

Cover design by Andi Kleinman, graphic designer, Flagstaff, Arizona

Website: www.therewasone.com
Website design by my PC Techs.com, Phoenix, Arizona

DISCLAIMER
The information contained in this workbook is not to be considered as legal advice. They are guidelines. **Each situation is unique and should be discussed with your personal attorney.** Always consult with an attorney or certified financial planner before making decisions that will affect your financial situation or when planning to transfer title to real estate. Consult with your banker too regarding your bank accounts.

FOREWORD

As a practicing elder law attorney in Arizona, I can definitely state that the number one mistake people make in their lives—people of every level of education, socio-economic status and intelligence—is failure to plan. While "seizing the day" and "living in the moment" are lovely philosophies of life, the unexpected happens so frequently that we may as well expect it, or at least prepare for it.

Just ask Charlotte Fox, who suddenly became a widow and had no plans, no idea what to do, and only grief and desperation to motivate her. What she did is amazing; she gave a gift to each of us.

Along with contributors from several respected professionals in various fields of expertise, she designed, wrote and produced, *and then there was one*. It is a workbook to help anyone and everyone plan.

Although it is designed to comply with Arizona law, the information it contains—and encourages you to gather—is applicable anywhere in the United States…and probably in the world! It is a salvation for your family and friends, and an amazing resource for you.

Once you have your life and estate planning completed (through the use of this fantastic workbook and contact with any experienced professionals you need to assist you), you can relax, let go of the "what-if" worries, and live a fuller, happier life.

If a slim, but beautifully thorough workbook, can do that for you, what's your excuse?

I recommend it to every client who walks through our doors, and all of our staff, too!

—Patti J. Shelton, Esq. (Retired)
Shreveport, Louisiana

Dedication

This workbook is dedicated to my wonderful husband, Gordon C. Fox—the kindest man I've ever known. What an honor and privilege to be his wife. He was a beloved husband, father, son, brother, grandfather and friend. His passion for life inspired people. He will always be remembered in our hearts and in our minds.

PREFACE

No one wants to think about the day they are going to die, but the ones you leave behind will be grateful if you do.

On a personal note, the music left my life at 4:33 a.m. September 28, 2003. My husband and I had everything planned for his retirement—but in our naiveté, no plan in motion for if one of us died. We were so busy living, we never planned for dying. When a heart attack suddenly took his life at the young age of 54, there was no will, no life insurance in place, and bureaucratic red tape prevented my husband's pension from starting for six months. The situation was difficult, and needlessly stressful.

We are not the only ones to not be prepared. Statistics prove that most people don't have a plan. This is a huge mistake, a preventable mistake, and one that I would love to help you avoid. If you don't plan ahead and put your thoughts in writing, the state, quarreling siblings, or a host of entities over which you have no control will make your decisions for you. In many cases, those who you thought were close to you will take your survivors to court. I can't impress upon you enough the urgency in which these matters should be taken care of. Keep in mind, when you're incapacitated or dead, it's too late.

Dying is a serious and complicated business. Most of us don't know where to begin. *And then there was one* was written with the help of professionals who are highly respected members of their professions. Since you are concerned for the welfare of your survivors, the guidelines herein will encourage discussion amongst you and your loved ones, and thereby reduce or eliminate most of the disorganized frenzy, injustices and mysteries that often—but do not have to—occur. Comprehensive checklists, worksheets, forms, and letters have been developed, so you will know what is to be expected of your survivors upon your death. It is a known fact that the frame of mind one is in after losing a loved one makes it impossible to function at a fully cognizant level. Having everything gathered together for them, will help your survivors focus on grieving, their loss, healing, and not having the burden of additional suffering and victimization that lack of planning creates. **It is an extremely useful tool for trusted friends and family members who want to help but don't quite know what to do.**

I invite you to hold my hand and allow me to help you navigate this complicated and overwhelming maze. In so doing, you will protect yourself, your family, and make the transition easier for your survivors during this traumatic and heartbreaking time.

Kindest regards,

Charlotte
Author

INTRODUCTION

M ost experiences with death and dying are crippling at best, but add into the mix lack of preparation, mass confusion, financial devastation, family feuds, exploitation of the survivor, together with a variety of other peripheral circumstances, and you have a situation that is paralyzing.

When I first lost my husband, my mental state was somewhere between a drug-induced coma and a nervous breakdown. Having been catapulted into a world of unknowns, I was unable to function, much less make all the weighty decisions that were presented. Few are equipped with the ability or knowledge to know what to do in the many situations that surface after the death of a spouse. Most of us are forced to grope in the dark and fumble our way through. With the assistance of numerous friends, and months of bereavement counseling, I survived the heart-breaking experience of losing my wonderful husband.

This workbook was initially put together to help those who are in the throes of grief manage the transition during the first few hours, days, weeks and months following the death of a loved one. Over time, it has evolved to include all the guidelines necessary to make your estate planning and other end-of-life arrangements necessary to effectuate this transition. These pages are filled with comprehensive step-by-step checklists, fill-in-the-blank forms, tips, and numerous other suggestions to help you work through the process of planning and surviving a loss.

As you skim through the pages of this workbook, notice the checklists on the first eight pages of Section One. This will give you a good idea of what the survivor can expect to encounter. Section Two is filled with forms that should be filled out ahead of time to assist with your burial. Section Three (together with Section Five), is jam packed with all the information you need prior to any portion of your estate being distributed. Section Four has forms for your health care. Section Five has forms that list all your assets. By completing this section (together with Section Three), your survivors will have easy access and knowledge of your assets. They won't have to wonder or remember *what* you have *where*. Section Six defines and has your end-of-life documents, and also includes forms to help you make arrangements for your pets and other animals. Section Seven has form letters for you to copy, fill in, and send. It's too difficult to do 'business as usual' during this heartbreaking time, so I wrote the letters for you. Section Eight includes suggestions to assist the survivor, together with many other ideas and thoughts.

This workbook is recommended to those who…

…have recently lost a spouse, life partner or other loved one.
…are married and want to have their plans in order.
…are single and want to have matters organized for their beneficiaries.
…are trusted friends or family members of the survivor. (The survivor *really* needs you now more than ever.)

…are adult children with aging parents, or a widowed parent.

…simply feel that gifting this workbook to a co-worker or friend would be helpful to them.

In any event, if you are concerned for the welfare of your loved ones, this workbook has been designed specifically for you. When someone dies, there are important matters to be addressed and unlimited decisions to be made. It is a very critical time period. Taking some time and completing the information within these pages is a compassionate gift to all those you love and care about, because the tasks that reveal themselves following the loss of a loved one, are unmanageable on *many* levels.

As you read through the workbook in its entirety, you will notice that all the forms herein have been designed to help facilitate the management of your business affairs. Feel free to make copies of the specific blank forms as needed, (permission given on bottom of forms), and remember to **keep a copy of any letters you write for your personal file prior to mailing**. If you have a computer always save a copy to your hard drive.

Again, it cannot be emphasized enough the importance of completing the information within this workbook as soon as you possibly can. Dying is a serious and complicated business—whether it be a lingering illness or a sudden tragedy—being prepared is your gift to your loved ones.

So grab a pen, brew a cup of your favorite beverage, and hold my hand as I walk you through this comprehensive guide.

Kindest Regards,

Charlotte

- *Plan Ahead*

- *Learn What to Expect*

- *Learn What to Have on Hand*

TABLE OF CONTENTS

SECTION ONE

SECTION TWO

SECTION THREE

SECTION FOUR

SECTION FIVE

SECTION SIX

SECTION SEVEN

SECTION EIGHT

What Others Have Said

So many comments and letters of appreciation have come in from all over the country, that I feel compelled to share a few with you for encouragement. Rest assured, as the following attest to, completing the workbook and/or attending a workshop, will be a blessing to your loved ones.

"Your workbook has sparked a lot of discussion among family and friends...all for the good. Thank you for the fine work you're doing."

—K.B., Hartfield, VA

"The book is essential! I started doing this on my own, but the book has much more in it."

—J.G., Cambridge, WI

"I have told many of my clients about this class. The information is invaluable!"

—C & D, Milton, WI

"Exceptional! Very important and helpful. Very well done—good speakers, great information. Thank You! Have started discussion with my lady friends."

—B.I., Madison, WI

"Beneficial for legal aspects, personal planning, and estate planning—you did great!"

—B.H., Murrells Inlet, SC

"The text is very beneficial. I appreciated the positive, personal interest approach of the instructor."

—K.H., Myrtle Beach, SC

"After reviewing the book and showing it to my son/daughter-in-law, I would also like to order two more books."

—J.P., Minnetonka, MN

"Thank you for your workbook. It has been a great help in trying circumstances. Thank you for encouragement, and sound information for dealing with the loss of a loved one."

—S.R., Tempe, AZ

"I am so impressed with what you have done. Your husband would be so proud of you."

—D.G., Sacramento, CA

"This was invaluable to my aunt when she lost her husband, and she recommends it highly."

—K.M., Green Valley, AZ

SECTION ONE

1

*T*his section is a series of comprehensive checklists for you to follow. They are in order of importance for matters that will present themselves in (usually) a sequential manner for when a loved one dies.

If you are using the workbook for guidelines to help you with your end-of-life plans, become familiar with the checklists—you will learn what will be expected at the time of your loss. You will notice there is much that can and should be done ahead of time in preparation for your death. You would be wise to get these tasks done as soon as possible.

The lists are broken down as follows, and offer within them, direction, instructions, and suggestions.

"Death is the end of a lifetime, not the end of a relationship."
—Mitch Albom

Additional Notes

A life partner or other loved one has passed away. You have already made decisions and carried out wishes regarding organ donation, and necessity for an autopsy. Now the rest of your journey begins.

First Things First

Whether you are a close friend of the survivor, or the survivor, the following is your master checklist to simplify what must be done following the death of your loved one. Use this as your guide to take care of situations that need the attentions of the survivor. As you complete each task, check (✓) it off in the space provided. Remember to use the **Perpetual Calendar in Section Two—Pages 45-48** to jot down your appointments and to follow up with documents that are necessary to order so you will know when to expect to receive them or otherwise follow through.

____ A friend or family member should call other loved ones and the family's spiritual advisor. Because of the nature of the situation, your memory may not serve you well. Use the Relatives & Friends to Call form in **Section Two—Page 41** to keep track of those who have been contacted. As individuals are notified of the death, make a note of whom you called, and check off the individuals on the bottom of the form as they are notified. Those to call should include other family members and friends, spiritual advisor, employer, doctor, hospice caregiver, financial advisor, life insurance companies, social security, and attorney (if necessary).

____ With the help of the survivor, fill out the Quick-Reference Form located in **Section Two—Page 25**, so easy access can be had when asked questions about the deceased and/or the widowed survivor. Information contained herein is required by almost every entity you will contact on behalf of the survivor. When the form is completed, copy and slip it into a plastic sheet protector, or paperclip, bookmark, or somehow identify for easy accessibility—You will use this form often.

____ Contact a funeral home for an appointment to make the necessary arrangements. See Funeral Arrangements in **Section Two—Pages 27-33**. Remember to carry out the wishes of the deceased and the survivor.

With the help of the survivor, complete the following forms:

____Information Required for Death Certificate. **Section Two—Page 39.**
____Information for the Obituary Column. **Section Two—Page 37.**
____Complete the information for Eulogy, Pall Bearers and Grave Markers, **Section Two—Pages 29 & 31.** If this information is filled out prior to meeting with the Funeral Director, less time will be spent in this environment while making the arrangements.

Additional Notes

and then there was one

____ Keep track of *Donations, Flowers, Cards, & Acts of Kindness to be Acknowledged,* using the form provided in **Section Two—Page 43**.

    ____ Remember to help the survivor write, address, and send thank-you notes.

____ *Keeping Track of your Business Calls & Contacts,* by using the form provided in **Section Three—Page 71**. Use *Form Letter #8* in **Section Seven—Page 225** to follow up your conversations.

____ ***Do Not Allow <u>Any</u> <u>Portion</u> of the Estate to Leave Your Possession and Do Not Give Anything Away.*** All bills, including the expenses for the funeral, are to be paid first, prior to anything leaving the home. As a friend of the survivor, be diligent when informing him or her to not give anything away. Secure all assets! All assets may need to be itemized, and may need to be appraised, so use the *Estate Assets at Time of Death* form located in **Section Three—Pages 91-97**. It is a good idea to help the survivor fill out this form to the best of their ability as soon as possible. Use a video camera and pictures to help inventory the estate.

____ As information comes in, complete the form *Estate Expenses at Time of Death,* located in **Section Three—Page 89**. You will list here any and all bills that were due at time of death—including all funeral expenses, shared debts, and separate debts.

____ If death was work related, contact Workers' Compensation.

____ Check your safe-deposit box and remove documents necessary to settle estate matters.

____ Cancel newspaper deliveries and magazine subscriptions if need be.

____ If you have stocks and bonds, secure a copy of the Wall Street Journal for the date of death. You will then have a record of the dollar amounts necessary for your estate.

Locate Documents

✓ Check off in the space provided as the individual tasks are completed and place the documents in a folder.

____ **Prepaid (or otherwise) Funeral** Arrangement Agreements.
____ **Will, Trust, and Estate** Records of the decedent.
____ **Retirement Plans** 401(k) and IRA information.
    ____ Call the Employee Benefits Department of the company that sponsors the plan.

Make note of any account numbers and contact persons.

_____

_____

_____

Additional Notes

____ **Pension(s) information.** Contact personnel. When calling the employer, request they send you the benefits package necessary to initiate whatever monies may be coming to you, the survivor. Make note of any account numbers and contact persons:

_____

_____

In addition…
____ Inquire regarding sick leave and vacation time decedent may have accrued prior to death.

____ **Social Security Number.** Locate decedent's number, and make an appointment with Social Security ASAP. Call **1.800.772.1213** for the office nearest you. See Section Three—Page 73 for additional information. Remember to put decedent's Social Security number in the space provided on the *Quick-Reference Form* in Section Two—Page 25.

____ **Birth certificates** <u>of the survivor and decedent</u>, (certified copies). Order certified copies of them if you don't have them on hand. Do this soon, as it takes several weeks to receive them. Mark the date you expect to receive them on the Perpetual Calendar provided in **Section Two—Page 45.**

____ **Marriage License—Certified Copy.** If you don't have one in your possession, order it soon, as it takes several weeks to receive.

____ **Life Insurance Policies.** Write or call your agent or the insurance company to obtain the death claim forms you need to complete and submit to receive any money that may be due you. Use *Form Letter #2* in **Section Seven—Page 213.**

____ **Automobile Insurance Policies.** If death occurred as the result of a vehicular accident, contact your agent and obtain the necessary claim forms. Use *Form Letter #2* in **Section Seven—Page 213** to write insurance companies if need be. If the accident was not the fault of the deceased, contact a good Personal Injury attorney to handle the wrongful-death case.

____ **Homeowner's Insurance Policy.** Contact your agent's office and inform them of your loss. They will make necessary changes.

____ **Health Insurance Policy(ies).** Inform them of your loss.

____ **Bank Statements / Financial Accounts.** Inquire of your banking institutions as to the existence of any accidental death policies if death was accidental. Confirm joint tenancy accounts. The financial institution will help you with the forms to transfer your joint tenancy account to your name alone. They will also require a Death Certificate.

    ____ Obtain new checks in your name only when you are able. See **Page 20** in this Section.

Additional Notes

and then there was one

____ **Financial Documentation** for stocks, savings bonds, etc. If the deceased had stocks in their name only, a Stock Transfer Agent needs to be contacted to transfer them into your name, or change it to another name. There is a charge for this service, but it is nominal and it will be done legally.

____ **Mortgage Records.** Use Form Letter #1 in **Section Seven—Page 211**, when sending in your payments. If your mortgage lender has supplied you with payment coupons, enclose one with your payment. If you are allowed to pay your mortgage with a credit card, a space has been provided for your credit card information in the letter.

____ **Deeds to Home** and any other real estate you own. Change Title when you are able. A death certificate will be necessary for the County Recorder's Office. There is usually a 30-day waiting period. Counties may vary. See Affidavit Terminating Joint Tenancy form in **Section Two—Page 63**. Read about a Beneficiary Deed on **Page 59 in Section Two**. Beneficiary Deed (form) is on **Page 67**. Consult your attorney.

____ **Call your County Treasurer Office.** Inquire about widow exemptions and/or senior freezes regarding your property taxes. This can save you money. Ask about qualifications and when you can apply.

____ **Vehicle Title/Registrations.** Remember, <u>you must wait 30 days</u> to change title to your name, or to put it in the name of your trust. Bring with you the Affidavit for Collection of Personal Property (if applicable). This form is located in **Section Two—Page 65**. An easier way would be to have a **Beneficiary Designation** form completed, notarized and stapled to your vehicle's title. These are available on the Motor Vehicle Division's website, **www.azdot.gov**, or obtain one at your local MVD office.

____ **Business Records** if you own a business.

____ **Earnings Statements** for the last year.

____ **Copies of the Last Tax Returns Filed.**

____ **Veteran's discharge papers (DD 214).** If deceased was a veteran, benefits are available. You may call **1.800.827.1000** for additional information. Refer to **Section Three—Page 75** for additional information, and if it is necessary to write and inquire about benefits, use Form Letter #3, in **Section Seven—Page 215**.

____ **Time-Share Deeds.** Contact Member Services at the resort where you own and they will direct you as to what is required. See **Deeds to home** above. *There is information on my website's blog about unloading timeshares.*

____ **Open an Estate account.** Everyone's situation differs, so speak to your banker. The one opening the account needs to be the Trustee or Personal Representative of the Trust or Will. A Death Certificate is required. Ask about electronic transfers and virtual banking. Your banker will be able to advise you.

Additional Notes

and then there was one

____ **Internet Accounts**. Please make sure that you make a list of your computer-used accounts/entities, i.e. bank(s) netflix, etc., listing your User Name and Password for each, to enable your representative access. Complete the form Internet Account Planning, in **Section Three—Page 83**. *As with your Credit Card list, copy this page prior to filling it out, and keep it in a safe place.*

Now that necessary documents are located

____ **File for Benefits** due you via life insurance, pension, or other private entities. Use applicable form letters in Section Seven if it is necessary to write to the various companies. Oftentimes a phone call requesting benefit packages for survivors will get things started. Remember to make note of the name of anyone you speak with on the form in **Section Three—Page 71**, Keeping Track of Your Business Calls. Follow-up letters should always be sent referencing the date, time and substance of the conversation. Use Form Letter #8 in **Section Seven—Page 225** for this purpose.

____ **Call your Family Attorney** for an appointment if you feel this is necessary to satisfy estate requirements, or for direction in these matters. When you call to make the appointment, you will be informed as to what documents you are required to bring.

____ **Request the Presence** of the trustee(s) of the deceased's trust(s), or the Personal Representative of the deceased's will.

____ If **Probate** is necessary, simply follow the instructions from the court, and your lawyer as to how to distribute the property. Sometimes there are unresponsive beneficiaries or ones that can't be found. Your attorney will know how to proceed.

____ After you have established **separate credit**, close jointly held credit card accounts. Married couples should have separate credit as well as their joint. This makes life much easier after one dies. Use the Credit Card Companies form in **Section Three— Page 79**, to help organize your list. Write to the varying companies using Form Letter #6 in **Section Seven—Page 221** to follow up your call. They may require a copy of the decedent's Death Certificate. In Arizona, you have a duty to notify creditors of your loved one's death. Check with your State's residency requirements.

____ **Inform Credit Reporting Institutions** of the death of your loved one to help prevent identity fraud. You will find these addresses in **Section Three—Page 81**. Do so once your separate credit is established. This should always be done in writing!

____ **Passport**. Inform the issuing office of the death. Use Form Letter #7 in **Section Seven—Page 223**. Locate the phone number for passport applications in the blue pages of your phone book. When you call, they will give you the address to mail the information to. _____

_____

Additional Notes

and then there was one

____ In addition, if you haven't already done so, remember to **contact your nearest Social Security office** for an appointment, and/or instructions to notify them of the death. See Section Three—Page 73. If you must notify their office by mail, send your letter *Certified Mail, Return Receipt Requested*.

____ **Notify the Internal Revenue Service** of the death. If you have an accountant, they can help you complete the necessary forms. If you do not have an accountant, contact the nearest Internal Revenue Service office and ask for the forms to notify them of the death. Send your mail to them *Certified, Return Receipt Requested*.

____ If you haven't already done so, **purchase a fire-proof safe** for your home, or get a safe deposit box at your financial institution for all of your important documents. Whichever you have—a fire-proof safe or safe deposit box—make sure those who need to know, know where the key is.

____ Have a trusted friend or family member **write thank-you notes** in response to the flowers sent, cards received, meals prepared for you, and all other acts of kindness on the part of others. Refer to the form you filled out in Section Two—Page 43. Oftentimes, funeral homes provide thank-you notes. Don't be afraid to ask. People and businesses will help if asked. Sample Letters are also provided in Section Seven—Page 227.

Complete Forms

____ Estate Expenses at Time of Death. **Section Three—Page 89.**
  Refer to the form provided for further instruction.

____ Estate Assets at Time of Death. **Section Three—Pages 91-97.**
  This information may be required if it is necessary to calculate the estate assets at time of death if the property is to be divided among beneficiaries.

____ Bills that Need to be Paid *Now*. **Section Three—Page 85.**
  With the help of the survivor, complete this form to help him or her understand the bills that need to be paid NOW. Watch for bills that will be coming in the mail. Note: No further payments will be necessary on life insurance policies following death.

____ Monthly Budget. **Section Three—Page 87.**
  With the help of the survivor, complete this form and list the bills that need to be paid on a MONTHLY BASIS.

Additional Notes

___ Credit Card Companies. **Section Three—Page 79.**
Follow the directions on this form to simplify the task of canceling cards that will no longer be necessary. If this workbook is being completed prior to the death of the purchasers, it will be an easier process for the survivor(s). Remember you need the maiden name of the deceased's mother, and verbal authorization from the survivor to act on their behalf when making the calls. Follow up any phone calls with a letter, using Form Letter #6 in **Section Seven—Page 221.**

___ Utilities.
Write utility companies notifying them of who is authorized to shut off, close, or adjust account upon your death. Do this while still alive.

Personal Health Care

If the survivor hasn't done so prior to losing their loved one, help him or her complete the following forms. This information is very necessary for the caregivers when helping the survivor after their loss.

___ Health Care Information Form—**Section Four—Page 101 & 103.**
This information is necessary to help take better care of the survivor. If this workbook is being utilized prior to the death of the purchasers, this information is necessary for all members of the household to complete. Having the information on hand makes it easier to provide for the survivor(s).

___ Medications You are Taking—**Section Four—Page 105 & 107.**
This information is necessary to help take better care of the survivor. If this workbook is being utilized prior to the death of the purchasers, this information is necessary for all members of the household to complete. Having this on hand makes it easier to provide for the survivor's current health issues.

___ Emergency Contacts—**Section Four—Page 109.**
Complete this form and somehow either mark its place, or copy it and keep it handy somewhere. Make it available for whomever you feel needs this information.

Additional Notes

and then there was one

As Soon as Possible

1

____ With the help of a professional, review your own estate plan if you had one in place. You may need to make some changes now regarding insurance policies, legal documents, and investment plans. If you don't have an estate plan, now may be the time to make one. Complete the Informational Questionnaire form in **Section Five—Pages 125-141** prior to seeing an estate planner, trust attorney, or elder law specialist. This will expedite your conference time. This will also let your survivors know what you have and where it is located.

____ Go to **Section Six—Pages 169-171** and carefully read the definitions and necessity for End-of-Life Documents. It's important to be educated and familiar with these documents. Complete your own end-of-life arrangements by filling in the applicable forms in **Sections Five and Six.**

____ When you have these <u>completed</u> documents in your possession, fill out the Wallet-Sized Notice form in **Section Six—Page 195,** and check all that apply. Remember to list a contact person and alternate before laminating.
____ Laminate this 'Notice' so it keeps well in your wallet.

____ Consult with your tax attorney or accountant. They will be able to guide you as to what needs to be done on your behalf with your finances.

____ Security. Give careful considerations for your safety. If you are a widow, you may wish to keep your husband's name on utility bills and whatever else you may desire. Your local police department will gladly give you tips for securing you and your home.

____ Additional forms to help you complete your own end-of-life arrangements are provided in **Section Five.** You will find extra copies of the Quick-Reference Form, Information Required for Death Certificate (for the survivor), and forms to personalize your funeral arrangements. If you purchased this workbook as a couple preparing your end-of-life arrangements, simply fill out the applicable portions of the forms provided.

____ If you have hearing aids or glasses and wish to donate them for the indigent, you may contact the Lions Club Sight & Hearing Foundation, **1.602.954.1723.** They will direct you to places that receive these items and give you a receipt for tax purposes.

____ Make provisions for your pet(s). See Arrangements for Pets, **Section Six—Pages 201-203.**

____ When in doubt...***don't***. It is common knowledge that making major decisions should be delayed for at least one to two years. It takes a while for our mind to think clearly again. Don't allow yourself to be forced. If you have the privilege of being able to wait with regards to selling your home, or car, or moving, or in making other major financial decisions, please do so. Please see **Page 124** for timely guidelines.

Additional Notes

By Deputy Joel Winchester
Coconino County Sheriff's Office

1

How it is Occurring and Areas of Vulnerability

*I*dentity Theft is a multi-faceted crime, which nowadays is pursued through a variety of media options. Some options available to perpetrators intent in stealing identities and following through with subsequent fraudulent activity are:

- Mail Rural Route Delivery Systems
- Special Delivery Systems (Fed-Ex, UPS, etc.)
- Telephone
- Internet
- Newspapers
- Magazines
- Posted Promos

As we find ourselves living in the "Information Age", it is becoming more and more evident that our personal, private and financial information is "out there" in various forms, and unfortunately there are increasing numbers of unscrupulous people—"hackers", who are finding unorthodox routes and accesses to such information.

One of the targets for Identity Theft and Fraud are families who have suffered the recent loss of a close relative, such as a spouse, child, grandparent, etc. One method used by a perpetrator intent on taking advantage of this situation would be to first identify the decedent and see what can be found out about them. Often there is enough information available through the methods of media mentioned above to allow the suspect opportunity to assume the deceased's identity and proceed along in a channel of Fraudulent Activity for a relatively short but damaging period of time before it becomes evident to members of the victim family.

Frequently we find that the Fraud Scheme is centered around an effort to obtain an immediate "payday" by means of a method or device to either draw funds from existing credit or bank accounts or to use the deceased's identification to open fictitious accounts in the decedent's name. In either case, resultant damage from his scheme can and usually does occur within a few moments to a few weeks in which the perpetrator feels relatively secure in a belief that their efforts will not fall under scrutiny. They know to "dump and run" and move on to another victim when activities start to fall under suspicion. Victimization in these instances can occur from anywhere in the nation or the world, as the scheme depends only on the information received and the speed with which it can process through the chosen method.

Curtail and Eliminate Potential ID Theft

With all forms of identity theft/fraud, I would suggest, "The best offense is a good defense". This means simply to anticipate and prevent an opportunity from arising, which is much simpler and less labor-intensive than trying to deal with a "Bad Guy" after the fact. Jurisdictional problems weigh in heavily when trying to prosecute the perpetrator *IF* you are lucky enough to have caught them.

In regard to the loss of a family member and subsequent efforts inclined to prevent a Theft of Identification and associated Fraud Schemes, the following suggestions might be considered:

- Consult with the family attorney.
- Contact your Social Security office and advise of the death. **Section Three— Page 73.**
- Contact your financial institutions and advise of the death.
- Contact the three major credit-reporting institutions. You will then have the deceased's identifying information recorded in the database for the Fraud Alert Program. **See Section Three—Page 81.**
- Report any suspicious account activities to your law enforcement agency as you become aware.
- Retain any and all supporting documentation relevant to your suspicions.

If the decedent lived alone, contact local law enforcement and have the address placed on a close patrol for the next few months—primarily during the intervals that the residence will not be occupied, and have the mail stopped or rerouted to a relative's address.

Your local law enforcement agency has volumes of information to send you upon request.

Additional Safeguarding Ideas to Entertain

- **Personal Checks:**

    ► Have only your initials and last name printed instead of your full name. If someone takes your checkbook, they won't know how you sign them, but your bank will. It is not mandatory to have an address or phone on them. Your bank will advise you of their guidelines.

    ► **Never** have your social security number printed on them.

    ► When you are writing checks to pay your credit card bills, put only the last four numbers of your credit card account number on the memo line.

    ► If you have Internet access and your bank offers virtual banking, use it.

- **Credit Cards:**

  ▶ Do not sign the back of them. Write "See Photo ID". Some entities require they be signed. If so, still write "See Photo ID".

- **Wallet/Purse:**

  ▶ Place contents of your wallet on a copy machine and copy both sides of each license and card you carry. Keep this copy in a safe place. You will then have all phone numbers necessary to report them if stolen. If your wallet or purse is stolen, cancel your credit cards immediately and file a fraud alert with the issuing card. File a police report immediately in the jurisdiction where the crime was committed. This shows your diligence in reporting the matter quickly. Contact all three credit-reporting institutions and file a fraud alert. See **Section Three—Page 81.**

- **Passport:**

  ▶ Copy identifying information from your passport and keep in a safe place.

- **Hotel Keys:**

  ▶ When you check out of a hotel that uses cards for keys, do not turn the keys in. Take them with you and destroy them because they have all of the information you gave the hotel, including address, credit card numbers and expiration dates on them.

- **Use your shredder**

Please visit my website at **www.therewasone.com**
and click on the **'blog'** tab for additional ideas and supplemental information.

Additional Notes

Quick-Reference Form—Page 25

Complete this form, copy, and slip it into a plastic sheet protector, or paperclip, bookmark or somehow identify for easy accessibility—You will use this information often.

Funeral Arrangements—Pages 27-39

Follow the directions and fill in all the forms in this section prior to going to the funeral home for your appointment. This will help make your meeting less stressful.

Relatives & Friends to Call—Page 41

Fill out this form as you make the calls to relatives and friends. This will help you remember who has been called and who still needs to be called. Don't trust your memory. It will probably fail you in this stressful time.

Donations, Flowers, Cards & Acts of Kindness—Page 43

Fill out this form as cards, letters, flowers, food, and other thoughtful acts, start flowing in to act as your source for thank-you cards. A friend can help you do this.

Perpetual Calendar—Pages 45-48

This workbook contains calendars for four months. Fill in the 'month' spaces, starting with the month your loved one died, and jot down notes for appointments, anticipated receipt of documents you may have requested, and other obligations you may soon have appointments for.

Know Your Rights—Page 49

Immediately secure the tangible property of the decedent. Don't let the family "raiders" take anything until all has been accounted for.

Estate Distribution—Pages 51-61

This segment defines the six ways that an Estate can pass in the State of Arizona.

Affidavit Terminating Joint Tenancy—Page 63

Use this form to put the family home or other Real Estate held in Joint Tenancy in your name alone. This form must be recorded in the county the Real Estate is located in. *Complies with the laws of the State of Arizona.*

Affidavit for Collection of Personal Property—Page 65

Use this form to collect personal property such as vehicles, bank accounts, or stock accounts held in the deceased's name. This form can only be used if the entire estate's personal property is under $75,000, and real estate is valued at less than $150,000. *Complies with the laws of the State of Arizona.*

Beneficiary Deed and Accompanying Revocation—Pages 66 & 67

Beneficiary deeds become effective on death of Grantor or owner of property and designate who the new owner is. See explanation on Page 59 of this Section. *Complies with the laws of the State of Arizona.* (Example Only)

In Memory Of...

Recently I was shown a custom memorial handout and considered it so touching, loving and profound that I asked permission to share it with you. Besides the usual information of the deceased, it included a short letter *FROM* the deceased that she had written beforehand. It read as follows:

> Dear Friends:
>
> Just a note to let you know that I'm passing on and to tell you how much I will miss my family and friends.
>
> I have enjoyed life and it has been such a pleasure to know you through the years. The time we spent, the laughter we shared, the adventures we had—through the seasons of life—were precious to me.
>
> You are so very precious to me. You are in my heart and soul.
>
> Love always,
>
> Patti
>

Don't forget to include other particulars of the death, services, and other requests on your custom card. For example:

Interment: ....

Service: ....

Request instead of flowers: ....

DECEASED

Full Name _____

Address _____

Date of Birth _____ Date of Death _____

Decedent's Social Security #_____Veterans #_____

Driver's License # _____ State of Issuance _____

Maiden Name_____ Mother's Maiden Name _____

SURVIVOR

Full Name _____

Address _____ Phone _____

Date of Birth _____ Social Security # _____

Date & Place of Marriage (if applicable) to decedent _____

Maiden Name _____ Mother's Maiden Name _____

FUNERAL HOME _____ Phone _____

Address _____

Name of Director _____ Contact _____

Location & Date for Viewing _____

Location & Date for Memorial_____

Location & Date for Wake _____

CEMETERY _____ Phone _____

Address _____ Contact _____

Funeral Date _____

Notes:_____

_____

and then there was one

25

Additional Notes

*I*t is unfortunate that most do not have pre-planned funeral arrangements and money set aside for our loved ones to bury us. If you are reading this workbook as part of your estate planning, now is the time to investigate funeral homes in your area and make your own arrangements. Get information from a reliable source and do your homework—research the company thoroughly. **BE AWARE OF ANY SURCHARGES THEY MAY IMPOSE.** If you decide to have pre-paid arrangements, (exercising much caution regarding pre-paid plans), keep these documents with all other important papers in a fireproof safe or safe deposit box at your bank.

If you personally have experienced the loss of a life partner, you know the difficulties you experienced with all the information and decisions that were necessary at a very traumatic time in your life. You will also know the favor you would be doing for your survivors if you make these arrangements ahead of time. On a personal note, I found out way too late about an organization called **Funeral Consumer Alliance**. I would have saved thousands of borrowed money. Check them out on their website, **www.funerals.org**. Their national number is **1.800.765.0107**. They will direct you to a chapter in your area.

Assisting the Survivor with Arrangements

Ask friends to recommend a funeral home. Even if you have lived in your area for quite a while, you may not have had a need to engage the services of a funeral home. Homes vary on many different levels with regards to prices that are charged and the kind of services provided. Local reputation in the community commands deep respect.

The first thing to remember is to **DO THE FUNERAL *YOUR WAY, UNLESS directives were given previously by the deceased and you are carrying out their wishes.*** Have others help you with decisions you can't make alone, but follow your heart where you can. This is a difficult, difficult time. Make sure you are surrounded by those who have your best interests in mind. It would be horrible to look back and have regrets over something you had control over and it didn't happen the way you desired.

When attending the funeral home to meet with the director, you will want to be prepared, and have the information with you necessary to complete the process in as little time as possible. Move ahead in this chapter, and fill out the forms provided for this purpose. Take the forms with you to your appointment.

Additional Notes

and then there was one

Funeral Services

Federal Law dictates that funeral homes must give you prices for their products and services over the telephone. When you call the funeral home of your choosing, ask for prices of the following:

• Funeral Services & Casket price range
• Cremation price range
• Fees for use of a limousine
• Ask for special packages that may be available

Veterans are allowed burial in a national cemetery for free. (Service members, and their dependents are also provided this service). If buried in a citizen's cemetery, the plot is free for both the veteran and spouse, but services are extra. This may vary state-to-state.

If your loved one is a veteran, contact your local Veteran's Administration to inquire as to any burial and funeral allowances you may be entitled to. All Veterans, are entitled to an American Flag and a beautiful headstone. If Memorial Certificates are available for a deceased veteran, order it as well as extra copies for family members.

Viewing

If there will be a viewing, please bring clothing to the funeral home that you want your loved one to wear. Keep in mind, it is best to have a high neck and long sleeves on the clothing you choose. Please also bring underwear. This clothing will not be returned to you. If it is a closed-casket service, bring a recent photograph with you to display. Photographs are also welcome if the casket is to be open.

I would like to wear: _____

Eulogy

List below the name or names of anyone you may want to give the Eulogy for your loved one. (This may vary between the different religions.) If you are able, you may also do this yourself. If you want to speak but are afraid you will lose your composure during the eulogy, tape record a message and have it played through the loudspeaker system of the church or funeral home.

Name _____   Phone _____

Name _____   Phone _____

You may want some of your thoughts expressed at the Eulogy even if you are not giving it.

_____

_____

Additional Notes

and then there was one

Pall Bearers

Choose people who were close to the deceased. Six are usually needed. Both men and women can serve. List some you may think of at the moment:

Name _____   Phone _____

Name _____   Phone _____

Name _____   Phone _____

Name _____   Phone _____

Name _____   Phone _____

Name _____   Phone _____

Cremation

Cremation costs will vary depending on services you choose to go along with it. When you call your chosen funeral home, prices will be quoted over the phone. Some funeral homes require a form to be signed. Please inquire of this at the home of your choosing. If the deceased is going to be cremated, you will be notified when you are able to pick up the cremains (the ashes). **Please do not do this alone**. This is very traumatic. Have a friend bring you to the funeral home.

Purchasing a Grave Marker

This may be done immediately, or anytime afterwards. There is no rush. If your loved one is a war Veteran or has an Honorable Discharge, markers are provided free. Your director has all the information necessary to order. Give thought to what you want the marker to say. Usually it states the Date of Birth, Date of Death, Beloved Husband or Wife, Son, Daughter, Mother, Father, Sister, Brother, Grandmother, Grandfather, Aunt, Uncle.

Keep it dignified, keep it brief. List some of your thoughts here:

_____

_____

_____

Additional Notes

and then there was one

Purchasing an Urn

The same rule applies as for the grave marker. You can either do it immediately—purchasing an urn from the funeral home—or if you choose not to, a simple container provided you from the crematory will hold the cremains until you are ready to purchase an urn from either the funeral home at a later date, or from any number of other businesses. You may also choose inurnment, where the cremains are placed in a special building at the cemetery, or a special room in a church. Your funeral director can help you decide what to do. Again, you don't need to make this decision immediately.

Flowers

Flowers may be ordered through the funeral home, or independently by you. A funeral home may charge for this service, so ask first. Put a trusted friend in charge of the flowers and decide on a budget ahead of time.

Florist _____ Phone _____

Purchasing a Cemetery Plot

Your funeral director will help you choose a plot if you do not already have one. He can also help you select a cemetery. If already purchased, located at:

_____

Music

Your church choir or funeral director can help with this choice and may provide live music for a nominal performance fee. List music you wish to be played at the services.

_____

_____

_____

_____

_____

_____

Live performance? or CD? _____

Additional Notes

and then there was one

Financing

Payment for goods and services are discussed with the funeral director when you meet to make the arrangements. They usually accept cash, check, major credit cards, verifiable irrevocable insurance assignments or financing through a financial institution. If you cannot afford a funeral, the County in which you live may step in and take care of things for you **if you qualify**. If you don't qualify for indigent services, and your finances are such as to create a severe financial hardship on you and/or your family, the funeral home of your choice may help you by offering discounted services. Your spiritual advisor should accompany you to the funeral home to verify your individual financial position.

2

Death Certificates

At this time, the number of death certificates that you need to order is decided. A good *average* would be **ten to twelve**. You get two for free if the deceased is a Veteran, otherwise only one. Over that, they are approximately $10.00 each. The following list will help you decide how many you may need. One is needed for each entity, and **you need one for your files**. They take approximately two weeks to prepare.

- Social Security Office
- Veteran's Administration
- Pension Benefits
- Life Insurance Policies—one for each company
- Real Estate transactions—recording new deed or deeds
- Banks. Each bank may require a certified copy. However, some banks are satisfied to see a certified copy, and will merely copy it for their files
- Safe Deposit Box
- Living Trust
- Credit card companies. Some companies have insurance policies built in. Remember to ask. You may not have to pay the balance if this coverage is provided.
- Vehicle titles/registration
- Home and automobile insurance companies
- Stocks
- Bonds
- Annuities
- Grazing permits on State Land or on the Reservations
- Any court-mandated situation in which you may currently be involved
- Don't forget to order one for your records

Additional Notes

Do you want your obituary in a particular newspaper?

If so, state here:

and then there was one

Information for the Obituary Column

Full name _____

Parents' full names (use maiden name) _____

Names and relationships of survivors

_____

_____

Date and place of marriage _____

Names of those who preceded the loved one in death

_____

_____

Chronological life history of the deceased. For example...where born; when moved to town; where schooled; years as a veteran, major accomplishments

_____

_____

_____

_____

Hobbies enjoyed by the deceased _____

Church affiliation and activities_____

Clubs and organizations your loved one was a member of, or formerly a member of

_____

_____

_____

Name and address where charitable contributions can be sent if so desired

_____

One Last Thought

In the times in which we live, and depending on where you live, anticipate the actions of predators who prey on opportunities afforded them. They read the newspaper obituaries and will know when your home will be empty during the funeral services. You may want to consider having someone stay at your home during the time you are away, or run the obituary afterwards. If you have an alarm system, use it!

Additional Notes

Bring this completed form with you to the funeral home

Name		D.O.B.	SS#

Date of Death	Age	If Under One year: Months(s)_____ Days_____ Hours_____ Minutes_____

City & State of Birth	Citizen of what Country?

Place of Death: □ Hospital □ Institution □ DOA □ Operating Emergency □ In-Patient	Town/City	State

If death occurred at residence, give address

Race: □ White □ Black □ American Indian □ Hispanic

If Hispanic, indicate: □ Mexican □ Spanish □ Puerto Rican □ Cuban □ Other _____

Was deceased ever in the U.S. Armed Forces? □ Yes □ No If Yes, bring copy of your DD214

Was deceased: □ Married □ Never Married □ Widowed □ Divorced

Surviving Spouse	If wife, give maiden name

Usual Occupation	Business or Industry	Education: Highest Grade Completed _____

Was death work-related? □ Yes □ No If Yes, contact your local Workers' Compensation Office

Usual Residence (Full Address)	Inside City Limits? □ Yes □ No On Reservation? □ Yes □ No

Father's Full Name	Mother's Full Name (Use Maiden Name)

Informant's Information

Print Informant's Name	Relationship to the Deceased

Informant's Signature	Informant's Complete Address

and then there was one

Additional Notes

Financial Advisor

Tax Preparer

Securities Broker

and then there was one

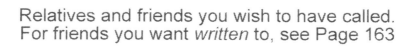

Relatives and friends you wish to have called.
For friends you want *written* to, see Page 163

2

Name	Phone	Contacted	Left Message

Remember also your...

Name   Phone

- Spiritual Advisor _____   _____
- Employer _____   _____
- Doctor _____   _____
- Hospice Caregiver _____   _____
- Life Insurance Company (ies) _____   _____
- Social Security _____   _____
- Attorney _____   _____

Additional Notes

and then there was one

2

As gifts and well-wishes come in from family and friends, list them here.

From	Description	Thank You

Remember to send *Thank You* notes

Additional Notes

and then there was one

Month _____

SUN	MON	TUE	WED	THU	FRI	SAT

2

NOTES: _____

_____

and then there was one

Month _____

SUN	MON	TUE	WED	THU	FRI	SAT

NOTES: _____

_____

and then there was one

Month _____

SUN	MON	TUE	WED	THU	FRI	SAT

2

NOTES: _____

_____

and then there was one

Month _____

SUN	MON	TUE	WED	THU	FRI	SAT

NOTES: _____

_____

and then there was one

By Leighton H. Rockafellow
Attorney at Law

2

Know your Rights as a Survivor!

It is highly recommended that the survivor contact an attorney familiar with estate law.

Do not allow any portion of the estate to leave your possession, and do not give anything away until the estate is settled. Coin collections, artwork and other personal items may have greater value than originally imagined.

- Nothing should leave the home until all funeral expenses and other bills/estate expenses are paid.

- Take an inventory and videotape the home "as is" with a date stamp on the tape. Narrate if you are up to it.

- Creditors take priority over heirs.

- Secure the assets. They won't go anywhere and division of personal property can wait.

Funeral expenses and creditor claims *have priority* over the rights of heirs.

Default vs. Decision

If *YOU* don't decide, someone else must!

—Property—

Default	Decision
Spouse (sometimes), Kids (sort of), Grandkids, Parents, Siblings, Grandparents	Any distribution you choose

—Health Care & Financial Decisions—

Default	Decision
Health Care Decisions—Up to the courts	You make certain decisions
Health Care Priority—Spouse, Adult Children, (Majority), Parents, Unmarried Domestic Partner, Siblings, Close Friend, Doctor	You decide who decides
Financial Decisions—Up to the courts	You decide who decides

—Minor Children—

Default	Decision
Guardian of Person—Up to the courts	You decide who raises your kids
Guardian of Property—Up to the courts	You decide who handles your children's money
Children receive $$$ at 18 or 21	You decide when your children receive $$$

Most of us would give our own life for the survival of a family member, yet we lead our daily life too often as if we take our family for granted.

—Paul Pearsall

Happy or unhappy, families are all mysterious. We have only to imagine how differently we would be described—and will be, after our deaths—by each of the family members who believe they know us.

—Gloria Steinem

Reproduced with permission from Jeffrey P. Hall, PLLC, Attorney at Law, 3115 S. Price Road, Chandler, Arizona, 85248

By Leighton H. Rockafellow
Attorney at Law

Securing personal property following the death of a loved one is a must. Resist the temptation to let family members persuade you to let them take items of personal property from the home "because he would have wanted me to have it." Inventory everything. Videotape the home, and provide a narration as to what is being shown on the videotape.

Don't forget coin collections, baseball card collections, china collections, or other collections that may seem trivial or useless at the time. It may be that they have significant value.

Nothing should be distributed until all assets have been accounted for, and all funeral expenses and debts have been paid. Arizona Law provides that funeral expenses and claims of creditors take priority over inheritance rights.

In Arizona, there are six ways that an Estate can pass:

1. Intestacy (No Will)
2. Written Will
3. Beneficiary Deed* (see below)
4. Trust or Family Trust
5. Joint Tenancy With Right of Survivorship* (see below)
6. Community Property With Right of Survivorship* (see below)

While avoiding Probate can be desirable, oftentimes it cannot be avoided.

The explanations that follow will help you understand the six ways an Estate can pass.

*Consult an attorney or title company for *any* deed preparation

Additional Notes

1. Intestacy

A person dies intestate if that person dies without a valid Will. All states have statutory methods providing for distribution of Estate assets if a person dies intestate. This statutory scheme creates a Will where none exists.

In Arizona, if a person dies without a Will, that person's property will be distributed to:

a. The decedent's spouse, unless the decedent had children from a prior marriage. If there are children from a prior marriage, 50% of the Estate goes to the surviving spouse, and 50% goes to the surviving children. Thus, if there are four children, the four children share 50% of the Estate. The remaining 50% goes to the surviving spouse.

b. To the children of the decedent, if the decedent does not have a surviving spouse, in equal shares.

c. If there are no spouse or children, the property then passes to the decedent's parents.

d. If the parents are deceased, the property then passes to the decedent's brothers, sisters, nephews or nieces.

e. If none of the above exists, to the descendants of the decedent's grandparents for up to five generations back.

f. If none of these exist, the Estate "escheats" to the State, meaning the property goes to the State, as there is no one to inherit the property.

Probate is not necessary if the total value of the decedent's estate consists of less than $75,000* in personal property and less than $150,000* in real estate. If personal or real estate values exceed either of these amounts, probate will be required. Assets with beneficiary designations do not go through probate. For example, bank accounts, insurance policies, homes with Beneficiary Deeds, etc.

It is recommended that a probate attorney be retained for this process. The Petition requesting that the Court appoint a Personal Representative (Executor) needs to be filed. If there is a Will, the Will should be filed, and certified to be the last known Will and Testament. If there is no Will, the Petition should state that there is no Will, and that none has been found after a diligent search.

Once appointed, the Personal Representative is required to send his or her Notice of Appointment to the heirs of the decedent, and to other interested parties, including creditors.

Notices are sent to creditors and published in a newspaper. Creditors then have four months within which to file claims. Claims not filed within that period of time are deemed waived.

The Personal Representative is charged with the responsibility of inventorying the Estate assets, paying debts owed by the Estate, and distributing the remainder to the heirs.

*Values subject to change over time

Additional Notes

and then there was one

If there is a dispute over who is an heir, and who is not, there may have to be a contested court proceeding to have the court decide whether or not the person is an heir or not. Unadopted foster children and stepchildren are not considered heirs under the law.

The Personal Representative is also responsible for the preparation of final tax returns, payment of any final taxes due from Estate assets, or distribution of any tax refunds to the heirs.

The Personal Representative is charged with the responsibility of distributing Estate assets according to the Will or as provided for by the laws of Intestate Succession should the decedent die without a Will.

Finally, the Personal Representative is charged with the responsibility of filing a final report and a Petition to close the probate, and request declaration from the Court that all assets have been distributed and the Estate may be closed.

2. Written Will

A Will directs the Personal Representative who is to distribute the property. There are three types of Probates available in Arizona:

      a. Supervised
      b. Formal
      c. Informal

a. A Supervised probate requires that the Personal Representative not enter into a binding agreement on the Estate or sell certain designated Estate assets, (such as real estate) or make distribution without prior Court approval.

b. Any Formal Probate requires that the Personal Representative obtain Court approval prior to distribution of property.

c. An Informal Probate allows the Personal Representative to take action on behalf of the estate without Court approval. However, the Personal Representative must keep the Court informed by filing appropriate notices and accountings with the Court.

The majority of Estates go through Informal Probate proceedings. The process of Informal Probate in Arizona is very similar to the process for Intestate proceedings described above.

Different states have different requirements for a Will to be valid as well as different requirements regarding Probate. You are urged to check with your local Court or attorney to ascertain the requirements of your local laws. The Uniform Probate Code, in existence since 1974, has made many things uniform from state to state. Information given herein is directed primarily to Arizona residents.

Additional Notes

and then there was one

Dying without a Will (dying Intestate), means that you trust the statutory scheme to distribute your property. This method is not recommended.

Dying with a Will puts you in control of how your Estate will be distributed.

Wills can be challenged. A challenge to a Will is called a "Will Contest". Will Contests are limited. Most Will Contests involve a "lost" or "forgotten" relative, or a legitimate relative left out of the Estate allegedly by "mistake". (If you want to leave someone out, do it intentionally in the Will—*Intentional Exclusion*).

Other ways to contest a Will are for improper execution; lack of mental capacity of the Testator at the time the Will is made; or undue influence.

Will Contests do deplete Estate assets, as the Estate must pay for the defense to a Will Contest. Oftentimes, settlements are made with the person contesting the Will to preserve Estate assets for the remainder of the heirs, not because the person bringing the contest has a legitimate claim.

Costs of Probating a Will

Costs of Probate vary greatly from attorney to attorney and locality to locality. All fees charged are subject to review by the Court. Unreasonable charges will not be approved.

Costs of administration come from Estate assets. Until the debts of the Estate have been paid or compromised, the assets of the Estate are not available for distribution. Any heirs who pay for the expenses of Probate or other administrative expenses do have a claim against the Estate for reimbursement of these expenses. However, a formal claim against the Estate must be filed.

Probate proceedings can take months or longer. By statute, Probate in the State of Arizona cannot be completed in less than six months. This is because of the four-month notice requirements referred to above regarding creditors, and potential creditors of the decedent's Estate, and the time necessary to process the claims once they are made against the Estate.

Until the Estate assets are distributed, they must be preserved. The Court may require a bond of the Personal Representative to make sure that Estate assets are not wasted. The cost of the bond is paid from Estate assets. The general rule of thumb is that a bond costs approximately 1% of the amount of the bond. Example: a $500,000 bond costs approximately $5,000.

Additional Notes

and then there was one

3. Beneficiary Deed

Something relatively new to Arizona Probate Law is the availability of Beneficiary Deeds. Beneficiary Deeds became available in 2002 and allow a property owner to pass title to real estate to a designated beneficiary outside of probate. They become effective on the death of the grantor and not before. They are very similar to bank accounts that allow you to designate who the account is payable to on death—commonly referred to as "POD Accounts." Beneficiary Deeds become effective on death of grantor or owner of the property and designate who the new owner is. Beneficiary Deeds can be revoked during the grantor's lifetime. The "old way" was to create a new Joint Tenancy Deed so the survivors of the decedent would acquire title by elimination upon death. The Beneficiary Deed is cleaner. The Grantor retains ownership and control during his or her lifetime whereas all joint tenants own the whole, which could lead to ownership/partition disputes during the Grantor's lifetime. The Beneficiary Deed eliminates that possibility. Beneficiary Deeds can be revoked at any time. The sample form has a Revocation example also. Title does not transfer until death of the Grantor.

4. Trusts and Family Trusts

Trusts and family trusts can be used for many reasons. Trusts can be used to protect assets. Trusts can minimize Estate taxes. Trusts can make provisions for long-term care, or provide for a donation to a favorite charity.

Trusts are complex legal documents. No one should attempt to create a family trust without the assistance of an attorney practicing within that specialty. Trustees have great responsibilities. Should trustees not perform as required, the beneficiaries of the trust may pursue the trustee for acts of negligence or fraud. It is suggested that only one Trustee be named. Co-Trustees may not agree on some issues, and delay the settling of the estate. Ask your attorney to expound on this.

Administering a trust requires that the trustee understand the wishes of the trust maker or settlor. A trust maker or settlor creates the trust.

Trust administration is determined by the provisions of the trust. Each trust is different, and custom-made to suit the wishes of the trust maker. Managing a trust, or acting as a trustee is a serious undertaking, and should not be accepted without securing the advice of an attorney specializing in this area of the law.

Additional Notes

5. Joint Tenancy with Right of Survivorship

Joint Tenancy with Right of Survivorship is a legal method of holding property. Bank accounts can be held in Joint Tenancy. Real estate can be held in Joint Tenancy. Titles to motor vehicles can be held in Joint Tenancy. Holding something in Joint Tenancy means each person owns the whole. Upon the death of one, the property interest of the deceased person passes to the survivor.

Filing an "Affidavit Terminating Joint Tenancy" notifies the world that one of the Joint Tenants has died, and title is now vested in the survivor.

Keeping bank accounts in Joint Tenancy allows persons to continue to use joint bank accounts even if one of the Joint Tenants dies. The death of one of the joint Tenants only means that the remaining Joint Tenant owns the entire account. The bank will not "freeze" a Joint Tenancy account when one Joint Tenant dies.

Generally, Joint Tenancy property passes outside of probate as by legal definition, the surviving Joint Tenant steps into the shoes of the deceased and now owns the whole property exclusively. No Court Order is necessary to make this transfer. Be on the safe side, and take your existing deeds to a title company to make sure they are written up correctly. Leave no room for them to be challenged by other survivors

6. Community Property with Right of Survivorship

Recently, the State of Arizona created a new method of holding title to real property entitled, "Community Property with Right of Survivorship". This is available only to a husband and wife. Joint Tenancy deeds can be issued to friends, unmarried persons, or business partners. Only a husband and wife can take title to a property as Community Property with Right of Survivorship.

On a co-owner's death, that person's interest ends, and cannot be disposed of by Will. The property passes to the survivor outside of probate. To accept the property as Community Property with the Right of Survivorship, this must be expressly stated in writing and accepted by both parties at the time ownership is acquired. A co-owner's interest cannot be seized and sold separately, but the entire property may be sold at execution sale to satisfy creditors.

The primary difference between Community Property and Community Property with Right of Survivorship, is that upon the co-owner's death, if property is owned only as community property with no Right of Survivorship, half of the property belongs to the survivor and the other half goes by Will to the deceased person's designated heirs. Holding property as Community Property with the Right of Survivorship insures that the property passes to the surviving spouse. There is also a step-up tax advantage when holding property in this manner as opposed to #5 above, Joint Tenancy.

Additional Notes

Make a copy before recording. Write down the date you recorded document here

and then there was one

Affidavit Terminating Joint Tenancy

The undersigned Affiant, being first duly sworn, states:

I am the surviving spouse of _____ , who died on the _____ day of _____ 20 _____ , in the city of _____ , State of _____ and who was then a resident of _____ County.

That, at the time of death, my spouse was the owner in Joint Tenancy with Right of Survivorship with me of the following described real property:

That title to said property was acquired as Joint Tenancy with Right of Survivorship by _____ as recorded in the office of the Recorder, Docket Number _____ Page _____ of _____ County, State of _____ .

A certified copy of the Certificate of Death of my spouse is attached.

This Affidavit is made from my own knowledge and I will testify positively to the truth of the same in any court whenever called upon for that purpose.

DATED this _____ day of _____ , 20 _____ .

_____
Affiant

STATE OF _____)
                        : §
COUNTY OF _____)

The foregoing instrument was acknowledged before me this _____ day of _____ , 20 _____ by _____ .

_____
Notary Public

My commission expires:

_____

Additional Notes

Keep copies of completed forms. List items collected here

and then there was one

Affidavit for Collection of Personal Property

I, _____ , surviving spouse of _____
the deceased, being first duly sworn, on oath deposes and says:

1. _____ died on the _____ day of _____, 20_____,
    more than thirty (30) days prior to execution of this Affidavit.
2. The value of all the personal property in Decedent's estate, wherever located,
    less liens and encumbrances, does not exceed $75,000.
3. Affiant is the successor of the Decedent, entitled to Decedent's personal
    property by Will or intestate succession.
4. No application or petition for the appointment of a Personal Representative is
    pending or has been granted in any jurisdiction.
5. Decedent owned debts or tangible or intangible personal property located in
    Arizona, described as follows:

6. The Affiant is entitled to receive payment of any debt due the Decedent and to
    receive Decedent's tangible personal property, or an instrument evidencing the
    transfer to Affiant of any debt, obligation, stock or chose in action belonging to
    Decedent.

This Affidavit is made pursuant to A.R.S. §14-3971 and §14-3972, as amended, for the
purpose of making claim to personal property of the Decedent under said Statute.

DATED THIS _____ day of _____, 20_____.

_____
Affiant, (surviving spouse)

STATE OF _____)
                          : §
COUNTY OF _____)

    The foregoing instrument was acknowledged before me this _____ day of
_____, 20_____, by _____, surviving spouse
of _____.

_____
Notary

My commission expires:
_____

Revocation of Beneficiary Deed

The undersigned Owner(s)/Grantor(s) hereby revokes the Beneficiary Deed recorded on _____, (date), in docket or book _____ at page _____ or instrument number _____ records of _____, County, Arizona.

Dated this _____ day of _____ 20____.

EXAMPLE ONLY
Do Not Duplicate

_____   _____
Owner/Grantor   Owner/Grantor

STATE OF _____)
                                               : §
County of _____)

    This instrument was acknowledged before me this _____ day of _____ 20____, by _____, as Grantor(s).

_____
Notary Public

My commission expires:

_____

Consult an attorney or title company for *any* deed preparation

and then there was one

Beneficiary Deed

I, (We) _____ , the undersigned Owner(s) /Grantor(s), hereby convey to _____ , as Grantee Beneficiary, effective on my/our death, the following described real property located in _____ County, Arizona.

Parcel Number: _____

Legal Description:

2

SUBJECT TO all liens of record, easements and otherwise recorded encumbrances.

If Grantee Beneficiary predeceases the owner(s)/Grantor(s), the conveyance to that Grantee Beneficiary shall either: ( ) Become null and void, or ( ) Become part of the estate of the Grantee Beneficiary. (Choose one)

> EXEMPT FROM AFFIDAVIT OF VALUE PURSUANT TO A.R.S.§ 11-1134 (B)(12)

Dated this _____ day of _____ 20____ .

_____   _____
Owner/Grantor   Owner/Grantor

STATE OF _____)
                                                  : §
County of _____)

       This instrument was acknowledged before me this _____ day of _____ 20____ , by _____ , as Grantor(s).

                                                            _____
                                                            Notary Public
My commission expires:

_____

Consult an attorney or title company for *any* deed preparation

Additional Notes

SECTION THREE

Additional Notes

Employer

Attorney

Social Security

Pension

Financial Advisor

Tax Preparer

Securities Broker

Health Insurance

Funeral Home

Life Insurance

and then there was one

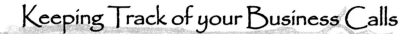

*F*ollow-up letters should always be sent referencing the date, time and substance of your conversation. Refer to your paperwork and/or business cards for addresses. Use Form Letter #8 in **Section Seven**.

Date	Business	Phone	Contact
NOTES			

3

Date	Business	Phone	Contact
NOTES			

Date	Business	Phone	Contact
NOTES			

Date	Business	Phone	Contact
NOTES			

Date	Business	Phone	Contact
NOTES			

Date	Business	Phone	Contact
NOTES			

Date	Business	Phone	Contact
NOTES			

Additional Notes

Contact your local Social Security Office for an appointment *as soon as you possibly can following your loss.* Take a friend. Timely application for benefits is very important.

<u>Back payments are limited to a 12-month period so do not delay.</u>

Your Social Security Representative will advise you and walk you through the process. Rest assured--any and all benefits available to you will be addressed.

There is a one-time death benefit of $255 that you will receive, if you are the spouse or a minor child who lived with the deceased at the time of death. You may also be eligible for monthly benefits.

Documents Necessary for Appointment

- Decedent's Social Security Number
- Death Certificate—Certified Copy
- Marriage License
- Birth Certificate—for deceased *and* survivor
- Divorce decrees from previous marriages
- Military service papers
- Your identification

A widow or widower can apply for survivor's benefits at age 60 or at any age if he or she is caring for an eligible minor (under age 16 or disabled). If applicable, ask how much of an increase you will get if you wait until reaching full retirement age. Minor children (under age 18, or 19 if they are still attending school) receive monthly Social Security benefits. If you are over 50 and disabled, you may also qualify for monthly benefits. If you are divorced from the deceased after a marriage of at least ten years, you may be eligible for Social Security payments. Your Social Security Representative will have all the answers for you.

To locate the office nearest you, call…**Toll-free: 1.800.772.1213**, or refer to your telephone book (blue pages) for the local listing under *Federal…U.S. Government…Social Security Administration*. At this time, you can also request the Survivor's Benefits Guide.

_____ Mark your appointment date and time on your calendar.

If you suspect fraud, Social Security Fraud Alert number is: 1.800.269.0271.

Additional Notes

Death Benefits

- Veterans Administration Regional Office...Toll-free   1.800.827.1000

- **Contact your local VFW or American Legion for gravesite services**

Life Insurance Benefits

- Department of Veterans Affairs
  Regional Office and Insurance Center
  Wissahickon Avenue and Manheim Street
  P.O. Box 7208
  Philadelphia, PA   19101

  Toll-free: 1.800.669.8477
  Toll-free Fax: 1.888.748.5822

  Website & e-mail: **www.insurance.va.gov**

Use Form Letter #3 in Section Seven, Page 215

- Office of Servicemen's Group Life Insurance (OSGLI)
  290 W. Mt. Pleasant Avenue
  Livingston, NJ   07039-2747

  Toll-free: 1.800.419.1473

Use Form Letter #4 in Section Seven, Page 217

Make note of the date your letters are sent on the opposite page, and keep a copy of the letter.

Additional Notes

and then there was one

*T*he following may be able to provide emergency assistance to widowed persons and their families, and/or guide you in the right direction for your specific needs. The list is general as each state, city and county has different programs with different titles. The best resource is your local phonebook. You can find them in the blue government section at the front of your phone book under County, City, or State Government. They will be able to refer you to other resources within your community. Your local Department of Economic Security would be a good starting point.

- Department of Economic Security—1.800.352.8168. This number will refer you to the nearest office in your area. Their hours are 8 a.m.–5 p.m. Monday through Friday.
- Community Information Referral—1.800.352.3792. Open 24 hrs. a day.
- Senior Help Line—1.888.264.2258. Website: AAAPHX.org.
- The American Red Cross
- Salvation Army—utility and rent assistance; food boxes; clothing
- Catholic Social Services (need not be Catholic)—money management assistance to people who receive Social Security Income (minimal fee). Emergency assistance with rent and utilities.
- Lions Club—eyesight and hearing assistance for adults. Exam and eyeglasses if needed.
- Community Health Center—sliding fee scale for health care.
- Share and Care Food Bank
- Arizona Food Bank
- Legal Aid programs

The first two numbers listed above can either help you or direct you to a source for help with rent, utilities, housing, food box referrals, transportation, senior services, medicines, vocational training and career center.

Keep notes on opposite page

Additional Notes

Please Note: It's a good idea to make several copies of this Credit Card form. This way, you have ample room to list joint and separately held cards, and have spares on hand for when the survivor passes. Important to keep this information in a safe place.

*I*n some states you have a duty to notify creditors of the deceased's death. List below the credit card companies you need to call, (listed on next page). Cancel the card if necessary, but also ask if the card could be issued in the survivor's name alone. If applicable, use Form Letter #6 in **Section Seven** to follow-up your conversation. ***You need to establish your own separate credit***. While you are on the phone, ***ask if there are any death benefits available on that particular credit card.*** The survivor should be close by, as you may need their permission to speak on their behalf with the customer service representative. In addition, they usually require the maiden name of the mother of the deceased.

3

Maiden name of decedent's mother _____

Card	Account #	Pin #	Customer Service Phone	Date called	Date canceled
Visa					
MC					
Disc					
Amex					

**To Help Prevent Identity Fraud, Secure a Copy of the Deceased's Credit Report.
Notify Credit Reporting Institutions of the Death Once Your Separate Credit is Established.**

Additional Notes

Date you wrote letters

and then there was one

*P*rior to reporting the death of the decedent, it is very important to first get a credit card in your name alone, (provided your own *separate* credit is not already established—as it should be). Begin by getting a copy of your credit report and see where you stand. In addition, order a copy of the decedent's credit report by way of the internet. (See internet address below). *Joint credit account history* will be reflected on both your credit history, and that of your spouse. Individual/separate history will not be reflected on the survivor's history. For example, if your spouse has an excellent credit history and you do not, you do not benefit. If you do not have a good credit rating, take steps to improve it.

3

Once your own credit is established, contact the Credit Reporting Institutions individually to report the death to help in the prevention of identity theft, or call the number listed at the bottom of this page. By doing so, you can confirm that the decedent's Social Security number has been 'flagged'. This happens once you have reported the death to your Social Security Administration. Credit Reporting Institutions are as follows: ***They do not share data with each other, so you must contact them individually.***

- **Experian (www.experian.com)**
  P.O. Box 9701
  Allen, TX 75013
  1.888.397.3742   **Fraud Alert Number: 1.888.397.3742**

- **TransUnion (www.transunion.com)**
  P.O. Box 2000
  Chester, PA 19022-2000
  1.800.493.2392   **Fraud Alert Number: 1.800.680.7289**

- **Equifax (www.equifax.com)**
  P.O. Box 105314
  Atlanta, GA   30348
  1.800.685.1111   **Fraud Alert Number: 1.800.525.6285**

Use Form Letter #6, Section Seven. Keep a copy of the letter. Send Certified.

Keep a copy of the letter. Send Certified.

Additional Notes

This same information will be required when the survivor dies.

Remember to include phone information with all passwords too. List below

NAME:	NUMBER:	PASSWORD:

and then there was one

By André Morris, President
my PC Techs, Inc.

*I*n this modern age, we use the Internet as part of our daily lives. If something were to happen to you, can your survivors access your information? I consulted with André Morris of *my* PC Techs in Chandler, Arizona, and he drew up the following to help your estate representative easily manage your Internet accounts.

E-Mail Account Information

E-Mail Address	ISP Name	User Name	Password

Existing Internet Accounts

E-Mail Address	ISP Name	User Name	Password
Google			
Twitter			
Facebook			

Website and Hosting Information

E-Mail Address	ISP Name	User Name	Password
www			
www.			
www.			

Additional Notes

This same information will be required when the survivor dies.

and then there was one

*L*ist any and all bills that are due and payable at this time, as well as those starting to come in the mail. This will help the survivor keep their finances in order. This too will be part of your *Estate Expenses at Time of Death*, Page 89.

Description	Amount Due	Amount Paid	Date Paid	Ck# or CC

3

List entity & addresses of your creditors here

This same information will be required when the survivor dies.

and then there was one

Monthly Budget

List Bills That Have to be Paid on a Monthly Basis

Description	Amount (a)	Date Paid	Check or CC
Mortgage			
Vehicle			
Vehicle			
Utilities			
Water			
Electric			
Gas			
Phone			
Cable			
Trash			
Other			
Child Care			
Food			
Medical			
Dental			
Other			
Credit Cards			
Miscellaneous			
Auto Gas			
Student loans			
	Total: $ _____ (a)		

Monies that need to be allocated on a monthly basis for quarterly, semi-annual or annual payments

DESCRIPTION	AMOUNT	Monthly Allocation	DESCRIPTION	AMOUNT	Monthly Allocation
Property Taxes			Health Ins.		
Vehicle Regis.			Life Ins.		
Vehicle Regis.			Medical Ins.		
Miscellaneous			Vehicle Ins.		
Miscellaneous			Home Ins.		
Other			Other		
	Monthly Allocation: $ _____ (b)			Monthly Allocation: $ _____ (c)	

Monthly Totals of (a) + (b) + (c) equals the minimum amount you need every month for your expenses

and then there was one

Additional Notes

This same information will be required when the survivor dies.

and then there was one

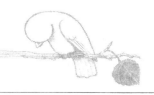

*L*ist the <u>bills that were due at the time of death</u>: *These include jointly shared debts as well as separate debts.* **This information is critical, as these expenses must be paid, acknowledged, and considered, prior to distribution of any part of the estate assets.**

Description	Monthly Payment	Balance Due at Death
First Mortgage		
Second Mortgage		
Vehicle #1		
Vehicle #2		
Credit Cards		
Visa		
Amex		
M/card		
Discover		
Mobil		
Utilities		
Miscellaneous / Other		
Insurances		
Funeral Expenses		$
Total Estate Expenses at Time of Death		$

Additional Notes

This same information will be required when the survivor dies.

and then there was one

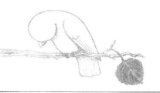

3

*T*his information is required if there is going to be a division of estate assets amongst beneficiaries. If that is not the case, you still need this information for an estate planner and for your survivors so they will be aware of your assets.

Residence and Other Real Estate

Location	Who holds Title	Estimated Value	Original Loan Amt. Interest Rate	Bal. due on loan
		$_____	$_____ / ___%	$_____
		$_____	$_____ / ___%	$_____

Bank Accounts: Joint and Separate

Name of Bank & Account Number	Type (Checking, CD, Money Market, etc.)	Name(s) on Account(s)	Balance(s)
_____	_____	_____	_____
_____	_____	_____	_____
_____	_____	_____	_____

Regular Investments

Brokerage accounts, mutual funds, etc. Please attach statements or separate list if available.

Item	Name(s) on Account	Value
_____	_____	_____
_____	_____	_____
_____	_____	_____

Additional Notes

This same information will be required when the survivor dies.

and then there was one

Money Owed to YOU

(Remember to decide if this money must be paid back to your estate, or if you will forgive the loan upon your death)

Description	Forgive the Loan? Yes or No	Value

Business Assets

Description	Form of Ownership Name(s) on Account	Value

Tax-Qualified Investments

(IRA accounts, tax-sheltered annuities, pensions, 401(k)s, 403(b)s, etc.)

Description	Owner of Account	Amount	Beneficiary

Life Insurance Policies

Insured spouse	Company / Agent	Policy #	Owner of Policy	Type of Insurance	Face Amount	Cash Value	Primary and Secondary Beneficiary

Additional Notes

This same information will be required when the survivor dies.

and then there was one

Assets with a Basis Significantly Lower than Present Value

For example, did you purchase your house, stocks or other assets many years ago for a price significantly less than they are worth now? If yes, please describe the assets.

Asset	Date Purchased	Cost	Current Value

Tangible Personal Property

(Motor vehicles, Musical Instruments, Artwork, Jewelry, Silver, Baseball Card Collections or other Collectibles)

Item	Location	Approximate Value
Estimate the total value of your household furnishings and other personal belongings	$	

Do you have any Burial Plans or Cemetery Plots?

Company	Type of Plan (Beware of Surcharges)	Price Paid
		$
		$
*Cremation?	Yes ( )	No ( )
Full Burial?	Yes ( )	No ( )
Where?		
Miscellaneous Information		
Miscellaneous Information		

*Remember…there may be required forms to sign if you wish to be cremated.

Additional Notes

This same information will be required when the survivor dies.

List your items here if you need more room:

and then there was one

Miscellaneous

Do you have additional or special items that should be considered in estimating your estate assets?

Description	Value

Summary of Assets—Types & Estimated Value

Description	Held in Husband's Name	Held in Both Names	Held in Wife's Name
Real Estate (residence)			
Real Estate (other)			
Rental Properties			
Bank Accounts			
Cash, Savings, Checking			
Dividends			
Promissory Notes			
Regular Investments			
Business Ownership %			
Limited Partnerships			
Tax-Qualified Investments			
Annuities			
Life Insurance			
Personal Property			
Bonds/income funds			
Stocks/growth funds			
U.S. Savings Bonds			
Miscellaneous			
Collectibles			
Other			
Other			
Subtotal	$	$	$
TOTAL ASSETS	$	$	$

Additional Notes

SECTION FOUR

4

Health Care Information Form—Pages 101 & 103

Two of these forms have been provided in case you have this workbook for your estate and life-end planning. Complete the forms for both you and your life partner. If you have lost your life partner, completing this form makes it easier for your survivors or caretakers to tend to your needs.

Medications You are Currently Taking—Pages 105 & 107

Where Are The Keys?—Page 108

Emergency Contacts—Page 109

This form is self-explanatory. It's a good idea to have this filled out in case an unforeseen tragedy befalls you. Your neighbor, good friend(s), and/or survivors need to have this information at their fingertips. Please make sure your loved ones have this readily accessible.

Staying Healthy—Page 111

This was written for your close trusted friend...to give him or her some ideas as to what to look for, and how to help you during this time.

Nutritional/Lifestyle Considerations—Pages 113-117

Dr. Timothy Munderloh of Flagstaff, Arizona, lists herein some nutritional ideas, suggestions about sleeping, exercise, and some basic stretches to relieve tension throughout the day for the survivor. As a close friend helping the survivor through this loss, it's a good idea to help keep them moving.

Guidelines for Personal Care—Page 119

As a caregiver, you might have put off your own health while caring for your loved one. These are general guidelines listing services that are recommended for your particular age group.

Additional Notes

Health Care Information Form

Blood Type _____

Name _____

Social Security # _____ - _____ - _____   D.O.B _____

Health Insurance Company _____

    Phone _____

    Member ID # _____

      Primary Care Physician _____

      Address _____

      Phone _____

Dental Insurance Company _____

    Phone _____

    Member ID # _____

      Dentist _____

      Address _____

      Phone _____

Pharmacy _____

    Address _____

    Phone _____

Local Hospital _____

    Address _____

    Phone _____

4

Additional Notes

Blood Type _____

Name _____

Social Security #_____~_____~_____ D.O.B _____

Health Insurance Company _____

    Phone _____

    Member ID # _____

      Primary Care Physician _____

    Address _____

    Phone _____

Dental Insurance Company _____

    Phone _____

    Member ID # _____

      Dentist _____

    Address _____

    Phone _____

Pharmacy _____

    Address _____

    Phone _____

Local Hospital _____

    Address _____

    Phone _____

4

Additional Notes

Your friends will need this information to help you.

and then there was one

Name _____

Medical Problem	Prescriptions	Dosage	Frequency

Over-The-Counter Drugs			Frequency

Special Needs: ( ) Insulin Injections   ( ) Prosthesis   ( ) Pregnancy

_____

_____

_____

_____

Additional Notes

and then there was one

Name _____

Medical Problem	Prescriptions	Dosage	Frequency

Over-The-Counter Drugs	Frequency

Special Needs: ( ) Insulin Injections   ( ) Prosthesis   ( ) Pregnancy

_____

_____

_____

_____

Additional Notes

WHERE ARE THE KEYS?

Vehicle

Vehicle

Quad

Motorcycle

Gun Safe

Safe Deposit Box

Desk

Fireproof Safe

Tool Box

Other

Other

Other

and then there was one

In case of an emergency, please contact the following:

Name	Relationship	Phone

4

Do you have a Do Not Resuscitate (DNR) form? [ ] Yes   [ ] No
Where is it located? _____

- *Advance Directives (Living Will)* located at _____

- *Durable Health Care Power of Attorney with Mental Health Authority* located at _____

- *General Durable Power of Attorney* located at _____

- *Last Will and Testament* located at _____

- *Living Trust* located at _____

Religion _____

Place of Worship _____

Address _____

Phone Contact _____

and then there was one

Additional Notes

By Sandra Gordon
R.N. (Retired)

*T*his is a time of enormous grief and stress. The body responds to this process by requiring more nutrients and care than usual.

If you are a friend helping the bereaved, take care to try to do the following:

1. Read the list of all prescription and over-the-counter drugs. Try to dispense them at the correct times and frequency. Check with the doctor if necessary. Be aware of any natural nutritional supplementation they may be taking also. Some can negatively interact with their prescription and OTC drugs.

2. Keep your friend hydrated. Plenty of water will replace the depletion of fluid that tears take away.

3. At this time, food is very important. Try to choose food with good nutritional value. You may find that not eating or over-eating (and perhaps drinking), may become a pattern. It's a good idea to keep close mental tabs on your friend's habits.

4. Keep your doctor and dentist appointments. Try to talk to your doctor. He has seen the grieving process numerous times before, and will know how to best guide you in helping your friend.

5. Get plenty of rest. Grieving is exhausting!

If you feel your friend is in need of counseling or behavioral help, local resources are readily available. Uncontrollable tears and a feeling of 'falling apart' are a natural part of the grieving process. These symptoms may last briefly or last a long time. Everyone is different. If your friend is coping at all, that is a good sign. However, if you feel things are not going as well as they could, ask the primary care physician to recommend outside counseling or whatever else he or she feels may be necessary to help the process. Hospice is nationwide and is an excellent resource for the grieving. Support groups and individual counseling are free to the bereaved. Grieving is a long journey, and it comes with repetition. Don't be concerned if your friend seems better for a week, then becomes anxious, or falls backward again. This is natural and normal for anyone who has lost a spouse. The loss is overwhelming, and emotions can rear up at any given time. Your friend may not feel like reading any materials for the widowed, but perhaps you can educate yourself first from books or tapes on grieving that are available at Hospice, the library, or at bookstores. This will better equip you to help your friend.

Additional Notes

Have a friend help you keep a diary of what you eat and drink.

and then there was one

By Dr. Timothy Munderloh,
D.C. DACBN, Be

S tress is basically what we feel whenever we are faced with difficult, unpleasant, or challenging situations. The way we deal with all this stress can substantially influence our overall health and well-being. Dealing with the death of a loved one ranks highest on the stress-level scale. Long-term stress takes a physical toll because the body tries to find ways to adjust to metabolic changes.

Seek the advice of your personal care physician before engaging in
any of the following exercises, nutritional recommendations, or lifestyle suggestions

4

- Be sure to obtain adequate amounts of sleep.
- Avoid sleeping on your stomach because it twists the neck and increases the arch in the small of the back. Stomach sleeping can cause morning backache, headaches, stiff neck and numbness of the arms and hands.
- Use a quality bedding set with emphasis on firmness and support.
- If you read in bed be sure to sit fully erect with pillows behind you to support your spine keeping your head directly in line with your shoulders. This rule also applies when watching television in bed.
- Exercise is critical when coping with stress. One should exercise for 20 minutes or more daily. This may include fast walking, biking, swimming or jogging. A target pulse range should be 185 minus your age. A general stretching sequence must also be performed for at least five minutes prior to engaging in aerobic activities. A five-minute warm down general stretching sequence is also recommended.

Diet can play an important role in helping to cope with stress. Eat foods that are low in fat and contain no sugar, white flour or additives. Eat a diet that is rich in fiber (whole grains, fresh whole vegetables and fruits), and is moderate in protein (fish, poultry). You should try to eat approximately 65% complex carbohydrate, 15% protein, and 20% fat and consuming very little artificial color, flavors and preservatives.

Drink ½ ounce of water per pound of body weight daily. This must be pure, clean water. Fruit and vegetable juices and skim milk are acceptable replacements for water. The discs of the spine are hydrostatic devices and require appropriate hydration for their efficient function. All the tendons and joints of the body are lubricated by a slippery substance known as synovial fluid which is composed mainly of water. Disc degeneration, joint disorders and tendonitis can be the result of too little water. Avoid beverages that contain caffeine, which is a diuretic, meaning it stimulates the loss of water from the body.

Additional Notes

Have a friend help you keep a diary of your exercises and stretches.

There are several nutrients and herbs that can be suggested by your physician to help one's body regulate and enhance their ability to handle stress and its manifestations. Research suggests that many supplements may help handle short-term stress and stress-related illness. Alcohol is a depressant and also impairs judgment. The use of alcohol should never be relied on as a means of coping. Use sparingly—in moderation—or completely avoid consumption.

Stress is a normal part of life, but when one loses a loved one, any prevailing physical or emotional conditions will oftentimes become exacerbated. It is a time in life when one must really focus on self, yet it is nearly impossible to do so. Seeking lifestyle modifications, exercising, meditating, counseling, biochemical and nutritional supplements can be very useful tools towards handling the stress caused by the present situation.

Some basic stretches to relieve tension throughout the day.

Neck

- Tip your head to one side as if you were trying to touch your ear to your shoulder. Repeat on the other side. Repeat three times on each side, holding each stretch for 20 seconds.
- Keep your body straight and turn your head to the side so you're looking over the top of your shoulder. Repeat on the opposite side.
- Clasp your hands behind your neck and squeeze your shoulder blades together. Now let your head fall forward so your chin is close to your chest, and bring your elbows together in front of you so they're touching. Pull down with your hands for several seconds, then release. Repeat six to eight times whenever you're knotted up.

Upper Back

- Extend your arms to your side and roll your shoulders as if tracing small circles in the air.
- While standing, try to touch your shoulder blades together.

Lower Back and Hamstrings

- While seated, extend one leg forward, slowly straightening your knee. As you feel your hamstring muscles in the back of your thigh begin to stretch, tip your toes toward you and stretch your calf muscles.
- Stretching your hamstrings. Sit on the floor with your legs straight and spread a few feet apart. Bend your right leg and bring the foot to your left knee. Then try to touch both hands to your left foot. Hold the stretch for 20-30 seconds. Switch legs. Repeat three times every day.

Additional Notes

and then there was one

Think Straight

- Remind your body what it feels like to have good posture. Stand with your back to a wall, your heels about six inches apart and three inches away from the wall. Place your arms at your sides, palms forward. Keeping your lower back close to the wall, straighten your upper back, lifting your chest and bringing your shoulders back against the wall. Tuck in your chin and bring your head back to touch the wall. Now pull up and in with the muscles of the abdomen as if you were trying to flatten your belly. Hold this position for ten seconds. Relax and repeat the exercise four times, with at least three sessions per day.

Pelvic Tilt

- Lie on your back with your knees raised and arms extended to the side. Press your lower back against the floor by tightening the abdominal muscles and squeezing the buttocks. Hold for ten seconds. Repeat 5-10 times.

Partial Curl

- Lie on your back with knees bent. Extend hands straight out between the thighs. Slowly curl upper torso until shoulder blades leave the floor, exhaling while rising. Hold for ten seconds. Do five reps the first week, then increase by five a week until you can do 15.

Spinal Extension

- Lie face-down on your stomach with elbows bent and fingers lightly touching your ears. Lift your upper body off the floor, exhaling. Hold for ten seconds. Do five reps to start, then add two a week until you can do 15-20 at a time.

Lower Back

- Sit in a chair and spread your legs apart so that your knees are beyond shoulder width. Lean forward, put your hands on your knees and rock from side to side to give your back a slight stretch. Next, lean forward and let your torso sink between your knees. Slide your hands down to your ankles and bend your torso to the left, touching your left ear to your left knee (or as close as you can get). Then raise your right arm over your head. Hold for 15 seconds. Sit up and repeat on the right side.

- Sit in a chair, cross your left ankle over your right knee. Twist your torso to the left, hooking your right arm over the raised knee and pulling gently. Turn slowly to the left, drawing chest to knee until you feel the stretch in the left buttock. Hold for 15 seconds and repeat on the other side.

Additional Notes

*A*s a caregiver, you might have put off *your* health while caring for your loved one. The following is a list of services that are recommended for your particular age group. These are *general guidelines*. Your primary care physician may want you to get these services more or less often.

TYPE OF SERVICE	21-64 YEARS OLD	65 YEARS +
Physical Exam	Every year	Every year
Blood Pressure Check	Every year	Every year
Cholesterol Check	Every five (5) years	Every year
Breast Exam	Every year	Every year
Mammogram	Once from age 35-40 Every year from 40 on	Every year
Pap Smear	Annually	See your PCP or GYN
Colorectal Cancer	Every year from age 50	Every year
Testicular Exam	Every two (2) years from age 18-39	Not required
Flu Vaccine	Ask your PCP if you're at risk	Every year
TD (Tetanus Diphtheria)	Every ten (10) years	Every ten (10) years
Health Education	Every doctor visit	Every doctor visit
Pneumonia Vaccine	Ask your PCP if you're at risk	Every five (5) years
Prostate Screening	Every year after age 40	Every year

Take good care of yourself

Additional Notes

SECTION FIVE

and then there was one

Financial Advisor Evaluation Questionnaire

A competent financial advisor can be invaluable to a widowed individual. However, many advisors are just sales people looking for a quick transaction. So it is up to you to evaluate and select the right financial advisor. To evaluate your current or a potential financial advisor, please provide them with this list of six questions and ask them to complete the questionnaire.

1. Do you have a legal requirement to fulfill a fiduciary duty to your clients?
   ___Yes　　　___No

2. Are you a Certified Financial Planner (CFP®) practitioner?
   ___Yes　　　___No

   If 'No', what credentials do you hold?_____

3. What is your method of compensation?
   ___Fee-Only　　　___Commissions　　　___Fee-Based

4. What services will you provide to me? Check all that apply.

   ___Budgeting　　　　　　　　　___Tax Planning
   ___Investment Management　　　___Estate Planning
   ___Insurance needs analysis　　 ___Education funding analysis
   ___Retirement Planning
   Other:_____

5. What documents do you need from me to do your work or analysis? (Please provide your list or write in the space provided)._____
   _____

Describe to me your experience in working with widowed clients, especially during the time period starting immediately after the death of a spouse and the two or three years afterward:
_____
_____

You want to find an advisor who is required to fulfill a fiduciary duty (by law), is a CFP® practitioner, is preferably Fee-Only, will provide holistic services (meaning they cover all areas of your personal finances), requires all your documents, especially your tax returns, to do their job properly, and has a reasonable number of widowed clients which they helped through the first few years of widowhood.

Provided by and reproduced with permission from
James Schwartz, CFP® CDFA™, RICP™, 8426 E. Shea Blvd., Scottsdale, AZ 85260

and then there was one

By Leighton H. Rockafellow
Attorney at Law

Once healing has progressed to the point of thinking about the future, you should make an appointment to visit an estate planner and/or a trust attorney. Take the time to fill out the forms in this chapter. Making your wishes known to your survivors will make the process easier for them.

If you are a couple, and planning ahead for the eventuality of death, completing these forms prior to your meeting (or prior to one of you dying), will be helpful in many ways. It makes both of you realize how much or how little you have to talk about. It helps the estate planner or attorney give appropriate advice concerning the Estate Tax and Estate Tax exemptions. It also avoids relying upon memory while sitting in the meeting. Meetings are usually where memories come up blank.

As unpleasant as it sounds, death is inevitable. None of us will escape it, yet all of us think there will always be time for planning. The time for planning is <u>now</u>.

- **Do not put off completing/changing Beneficiary Designation Forms, on a life insurance policy if that is what you want to do.**

- **Do not put off updating your Will or your Family Trust if it needs to be done.**

5

If sickness comes, take care of the sickness first, but take care of your affairs as well. It is an act of kindness and compassion that your survivors will appreciate.

If you die without a Will, the State of Arizona has a statutory plan in place. The statutory plan designates how the Estate is distributed. If you want to avoid the State making your decisions for you, make sure that you have an up-to-date Will that properly spells out your desires regarding distribution of property.

None of us can escape death. All of us can plan ahead to make dealing with our deaths easier for our survivors.

Completing this section, together with **Section Three, Pages 91-97**, as part of your estate plan either before losing a loved one or after, enables your heirs/survivors easy access and knowledge of your assets. They won't have to wonder or remember what you have where.

Please note: Some pension benefits may discontinue if the surviving spouse remarries. Check with your plan administrator or legal advisor for this determination prior to remarriage.

Timely Financial and Tax Decisions

*T*he advice heard by all widowed individuals, *"Don't Make any Significant Changes for at Least One Year"* can be harmful if followed blindly. Make sure your financial advisor addresses the issues which affect you, in a timely manner, to maximize your financial benefits and opportunities. Not all of these items affect every person. Many of these items require a decision by a specific date or length of time.

1. Continue paying your health insurance premiums to maintain coverage.
2. Claim Social Security survivor benefits after evaluating your best claiming strategy.
3. Assess living expenses and build a spending plan to know what you can or cannot spend.
4. Diversify an overly aggressive investment portfolio to prevent excessive losses.
5. Sell or move out of your home if you can't afford it.
6. If you do sell the house, you may need to sell it within two years of the date of death to take advantage of a higher exclusion to capital gains ($500,000 vs. $250,000).
7. Update investment, retirement, annuity, and life insurance beneficiary designations.
8. File IRS Form 706, Estate Tax return, if necessary.
9. Review your income tax returns and evaluate tax carry forwards such as Net Operating Losses and Capital Losses for planning opportunities before they expire.
10. Update cost basis for investments in taxable accounts to avoid double taxation of gains.
11. Understand your options related to your spouse's Employee Stock Ownership Plan.
12. Exercise spouse's employee stock options prior to expiration.
13. Take required minimum distribution from your spouse's IRAs to avoid a 50% IRS penalty.
14. Split an inherited IRA by December 31st of the year after the death if there is more than one beneficiary.
15. Disclaim property by the 9th month after the date of death. (Consult with your estate planning attorney on this issue.)

NOTE: Do not interpret this list as personal investment advice. Each individual must consult a competent advisor to evaluate their own personal situation.

Provided by and reproduced with permission from
James Schwartz, CFP® CDFA™, RICP™, 8426 E. Shea Blvd., Scottsdale, AZ 85260

and then there was one

Informational Questionnaire

Personal Planner_____
Phone _____
Appt. Date _____ Time _____

Date: _____

Prior to meeting with your estate planner, please complete the following information. Bring this form, (or the whole workbook), together with the Estate Assets at time of Death, (Section Three, Pages 91-97), and Determining Your Human Life Value (Section Five, Page 143), to the meeting. Doing so will better equip your planner, and your conference time will move along in an expeditious manner.

Name _____ DOB _____ SS# _____ - __ - _____

Address _____ E-mail _____

_____ County _____

Phone: Home _____ Business _____

Cell _____

Marital Status ( ) Single ( ) Widowed ( ) Married   Date of Marriage _____

Occupation: _____

Name _____ DOB _____ SS# _____ - __ - _____

Address _____ E-mail _____

_____ County _____

Phone: Home _____ Business _____

Cell _____

Marital Status ( ) Single ( ) Widowed ( ) Married   Date of Marriage _____

Occupation: _____

Tip: Use a Pencil where information is subject to change

and then there was one

Additional Notes

If Beneficiary is other than a dependent, state relationship, i.e.: friend, charity, other relative, etc.

and then there was one

Dependents / Beneficiaries

Name _____

Date of Birth _____

Address _____

_____

Phone _____

Dependent / Beneficiary of
( ) Husband   ( ) Wife   ( ) Both

Social Security #: _____

Marital Status _____

Name of Spouse _____

Name _____

Date of Birth _____

Address _____

_____

Phone _____

Dependent / Beneficiary of
( ) Husband   ( ) Wife   ( ) Both

Social Security #: _____

Marital Status _____

Name of Spouse _____

Name _____

Date of Birth _____

Address _____

_____

Phone _____

Dependent / Beneficiary of
( ) Husband   ( ) Wife   ( ) Both

Social Security #: _____

Marital Status _____

Name of Spouse _____

Name _____

Date of Birth _____

Address _____

_____

Phone _____

Dependent / Beneficiary of
( ) Husband   ( ) Wife   ( ) Both

Social Security #: _____

Marital Status _____

Name of Spouse _____

Name _____

Date of Birth _____

Address _____

_____

Phone _____

Dependent / Beneficiary of
( ) Husband   ( ) Wife   ( ) Both

Social Security #: _____

Marital Status _____

Name of Spouse _____

5

Additional Notes

This same information will be required when the survivor dies

and then there was one

Are you supporting an elderly parent?   ___Yes   ___No

Special Needs

Do you or any of your dependents have an illness, disability, or special needs, which should be considered in planning your estate?   ___Yes   ___No

What is the approximate monthly obligation to support the special need? $_____

Please describe the special needs below. Attach additional sheets if necessary.

_____

_____

_____

_____

_____

Other Persons who are Important to your Estate Plan

Grandchildren, siblings, nieces, nephews and friends, etc.

Name	Relationship
_____	_____
_____	_____
_____	_____
_____	_____
_____	_____
_____	_____

Is there anyone important to your Estate Plan (including your spouse) who is not a citizen of the United States?   List Name(s)

_____

_____

Additional Notes

This same information will be required when the survivor dies

and then there was one

Who do you want to handle *FINANCIAL* decisions for you in the event of a disability?

We will need addresses and phone numbers for these persons if not listed elsewhere.

Primary _____   Address _____

Phone _____   _____

Alternate _____   Address _____

Phone _____   _____

Who do you want to handle *MEDICAL* decisions for you in the event of a disability?

We will need addresses and phone numbers for these persons if not listed elsewhere.

Primary _____   Address _____

Phone _____   _____

Alternate _____   Address _____

Phone _____   _____

Trustee

Who would you name to be responsible for managing the funds in the trusts for your children? These trusts are scheduled (unless you indicate otherwise) to distribute out when your youngest child attains the age of 35 years. Since this trusted role may continue for that length of time, please consider your nominations and alternatives carefully.

Primary _____   Address _____

Phone _____   _____

Alternate _____   Address _____

Phone _____   _____

Additional Notes

This same information will be required when the survivor dies

and then there was one

Schedule of Distribution for Children's Trusts

Please indicate your preferred schedule of distribution here.

_____

_____

_____

_____

Guardian

Whom would you name to care for your children if both parents died while the children were still young?

Primary _____ Address _____

   Phone _____ _____

Alternate _____ Address _____

   Phone _____ _____

5

General Information

Please bring Copies of All Important Documents

	Husband (Yes or No)	Wife (Yes or No)
• Do you have a Will?	_____	_____
• Have you ever made a Trust? (e.g. Revocable Living Trust)	_____	_____
• Has anyone ever made a Trust for you?	_____	_____
• Are you a Veteran of the U.S. Military?	_____	_____
• Have you signed a Power of Attorney?	_____	_____
• Are your End-of-Life Documents completed?	_____	_____

Additional Notes

This same information will be required when the survivor dies

and then there was one

Health Care

Name and Address of your regular physician _____

_____

Do you have Medicare?   ___Yes   ___No

Do you have Supplemental Insurance?   ___Yes   ___No

   If so, name of Company and Policy Number:

_____

_____

Do you have Long Term Health Care Insurance?   ___Yes   ___No

   If so, name of Company and Policy Number:

_____

_____

Unusual Expenses

Do you have any Unusual Expenses that should be considered in planning your estate
other than for special needs as outlined previously?

_____

_____

_____

_____

_____

_____

_____

_____

_____

_____

_____

_____

Additional Notes

This same information will be required when the survivor dies

and then there was one

Income

Please list your estimated *monthly* income from the following sources:

Source	Husband	Wife
Social Security		
Interest		
Dividends		
Pension Benefits **		
Pension Benefits **		
Employment		
Employment		
Rental Income		
Stocks *		
Other Income		
Other Income		
Subtotal:	$	$
Combined Total Income	$	$

- Husband: Do you have a current Social Security estimate statement?   ___Yes   ___No

- Wife   : Do you have a current Social Security estimate statement?   ___Yes   ___No

*Secure a copy of the *Wall Street Journal* for the day of death so you have that day's rates for your stocks and bonds. You will need this for your *Estate Assets at Time of Death*.

** *Some pension benefits may discontinue if the surviving spouse remarries. Check with your plan administrator or legal advisor for this determination prior to remarriage.*

Additional Notes

This same information will be required when the survivor dies

and then there was one

Key Financial Advisors

Do you have any of the following? If so, please give name and phone number of individual.

Accountant/Tax Preparer_____

Securities Broker_____

Insurance Agent _____

Financial/Retirement Planner_____

Family attorney _____

Other_____

Safe Deposit Box and Bank Account Information

Bank	Branch	Account Number
_____	_____	_____
_____	_____	_____
_____	_____	_____
_____	_____	_____

✓ Do your bank accounts have a 'Pay on Death' or 'Transfer on Death' beneficiary designation?
If not, speak with your banker. This will help your survivor(s).

Do you expect to receive an inheritance or gift from any source that should be considered in your estate? If 'yes', describe …

_____

_____

_____

_____

_____

Additional Notes

This same information will be required when the survivor dies

and then there was one

Liabilities

Please list any outstanding liabilities if not shown elsewhere. You do not need to include ordinary monthly expenses.

_____

_____

_____

_____

_____

_____

Disposition of Assets and other Personal Property

To whom do you wish to leave items of personal property? You should consider making a list of such gifts and bring it with you to your meeting. In **Section Six, Pages 197 & 199** you will find Instructions for the use of, _and the_ Memorandum for Distribution of Tangible Personal Property.

Please include names, addresses, dates of birth, and social security numbers of all beneficiaries if you haven't done so already within this form.

Note

Please bring the following documents to your meeting if available and applicable:

- Will(s)
- End-of-Life Documents
- Deed(s) to residence/properties
- Latest tax return
- Insurance policies
- Bank or brokerage account statements
- Any other documents or information you deem relevant

Additional Notes

This same information will be required when the survivor dies

and then there was one

By Martin E. Battock
Financial Planner

One would never dream of being without Home Insurance, Car Insurance, Personal Liability Insurance, or Health Insurance. But when it comes to Life Insurance, and determining our Human Life Value, we tend to put it off, or disregard it altogether.

The following questionnaire will help you and your insurance advisor determine if you either require life insurance, or additional life insurance at this point in your life.

Total annual income before taxes...$_____

Average percent of salary increases assumed for

    all the years until retirement..................................... _____ %

How many years until you plan to retire?.............................. _____

Combined tax rate (State & Federal) .... _____ %

How much do you spend on yourself annually?

    Consider the cost of food, clothing, entertainment,

    & medical expenses. (Monthly figure X's 12 =)...............$ _____

How much would your family have to pay in premiums

    to replace the health insurance from your employment?.......$_____

How much would it cost your family on an annual basis

    to replace the household chores you do in case of

    your premature death?..$_____

Reasonable percentage rate of return that your

    family could count on each year upon your death.............. _____%

How much life insurance do you currently have?........................$_____

Following is a formula to help you visualize how you currently stand in the Life Insurance area.

A. Life Insurance you currently have $_____

B. Your annual income $_____

C. Now divide **"A" by "B"** to see the number of years

    your current life insurance would replace your

    current annual earnings   _____ # of years

D. How many years until you plan to retire?   _____ # of years

If **"D"** is higher than **"C"**, your family may not be protected against the loss of your income.

Additional Notes

By Martin E. Battock
Financial Planner

Now that you have determined your own "Human Life Value", you should consider protecting that value through the purchase of life insurance. There are four generally recognized forms of life insurance:

- Term
- Whole Life, or Permanent
- Variable
- Universal

Term

Term Life Insurance covers a specific period of time and holds no value once the policy period has ended. By way of example, if you purchase $250,000 Term Life Insurance for twenty years, life insurance protection expires at the end of twenty years, has no cash value, and pays nothing unless the person whose life is insured under the policy dies during the term of the policy. Term Insurance is generally best when you need a large death benefit for a temporary period of time with limited resources to pay premiums.

Term Insurance is initially less expensive in relationship to Whole Life, Variable or Universal Life. However, Term Life Insurance becomes more expensive as we age. Understandably, a twenty-year Term Life Insurance on a person age 60 would cost much more than a twenty-year life insurance policy on a person age 40. The insurance companies do their homework. They know the statistics, and they know the average life expectancies of people by age, gender and even geographical location.

Whole Life, or Permanent Insurance

While initially more expensive, Whole Life policies may become paid up at age 65 or sooner. These policies build guaranteed cash value and are projected to pay dividends. Generally, after fifteen or twenty years, dividends may be sufficient to pay policy premiums. At retirement, the policyholder usually has an election to make.

1. The policyholder can surrender the policy for its cash value.
2. The policyholder can elect to purchase a permanent life insurance policy for a specific amount with the accumulated cash value and dividends, or
3. The person may elect an annuity payment.

and then there was one

Additional Notes

Cash Value Accumulations in Whole Life policy cash values are not taxable during the period of accumulation. However, if the person surrenders the policy, or elects an annuity, any gains get taxed as income as the proceeds are received.

Variable Life Insurance

Variable Life Insurance pegs its cash value to various mutual funds, which you elect based on your investment objectives and risk profile. Variable policies have the potential to earn a higher cash value than Whole Life, but they carry a higher degree of risk. Once again, upon retirement, the policyholder, if living, can choose the options of paid-up insurance, a lump-sum cash settlement, or annuity.

Universal Life

Universal Life Insurance is for people who desire permanent insurance like Whole Life, but are less concerned about building cash value. As a result, the premiums are lower than Whole Life. When considering a Universal Life policy, it is critically important to purchase a policy that has a guarantee that your policy cannot lapse as long as you pay the required premium. Without this guarantee, you run the risk that your policy will require substantially higher premiums in later years or may even lapse before you die.

Life Insurance policies are important not only for the primary wage earner in the family, but for all other family members as well. Non-working spouses still have a significant Human Life Value. Protecting that value through life insurance provides a security blanket to the family that he or she may leave behind.

The same holds true for children. Children have a significant Human Life Value. Losing a child is a devastating event that can impact a person's earning capacity. Insuring your children for a sufficient amount to pay for funeral expenses, and at least six months absence from work is highly recommended.

Once again, the choice can be made between Term, Whole Life, Variable Life, or Universal Life. You are urged to consult with your insurance advisor regarding which product fits your needs best.

Additional Notes

and then there was one

When you are healed to the point of wanting to lessen the painful task of having your survivors make funeral arrangements for you, then it will be time to complete the following few pages. This is not a pleasant task, but may be less daunting for you than your loved ones. This will also give them peace of mind that your final arrangements are being done *your* way and not left for them to squabble about with any siblings who may not share the same ideas, or with your Personal Representative, or whomever you may have appointed to carry out your wishes. This is a kind approach to a sad situation. If you do not wish to purchase a pre-paid funeral package, perhaps simply inquiring as to the cost of your final arrangements and having the money set aside would suffice. Your loved ones will thank you many times over no matter which decision you make.

Funeral Services

As you did when you made arrangements for your loved one, call the funeral home of your choosing, and ask for prices of the following:

- Funeral services
- Casket price-range. Cremation price-range
- Fees for use of a limousine
- Ask for special packages that may be available

Viewing

If there will be a viewing, and you want to choose your own clothing, then do so. Keep in mind it is best to have a high neck and long sleeves on whatever you choose. If you have a favorite picture of yourself, let this be known, as this could be exhibited at your viewing. If you so desire, have copies made to pass out to friends attending the funeral. Have a larger photograph, perhaps an 8" x 10" made to display with the casket at the viewing.

I would like to wear: _____

Additional Notes

Eulogy

List below the name or names of anyone you may want to give your Eulogy. You may have one speak, or several. As many as may want to speak may do so.

Name _____   Phone _____

Name _____   Phone _____

You may want some of your thoughts expressed at your Eulogy.

_____

_____

_____

_____

_____

Pall Bearers

5

Choose people who you would like to serve as Pall Bearers. Six are usually needed. Both men and women can serve. List here some that you may think of at the moment.

Name _____   Phone _____

Name _____   Phone _____

Name _____   Phone _____

Name _____   Phone _____

Name _____   Phone _____

Name _____   Phone _____

Additional Notes

and then there was one

Cremation

If you wish to be cremated, keep in mind that costs will vary depending on services you choose to go along with it. When you call your chosen funeral home, they will give you prices over the phone. Remember, there may be a required form for you to sign if you wish cremation.

Purchasing a Grave Marker

This may be done now, or leave it up to your survivors. There is no rush. Remember that if you are a war Veteran, or have an Honorable Discharge, markers are provided free. Your director has all the information necessary to order them. Give thought to what you want the marker to say. Usually it states the Date of Birth, Date of Death, Beloved Husband or Wife, Son, Daughter, Mother, Father, Sister, Brother, Grandmother, Grandfather, Aunt, Uncle.

List here some thoughts that you may want on your marker, or leave blank if you wish to leave this up to your survivors. It should be brief and dignified.

_____

_____

_____

5

Purchasing an Urn

The same rule applies as for the grave marker. You can either do it immediately— purchasing an urn from the funeral home—or leave this decision up to your survivors.

Flowers

Flowers for any service you elect may be part of any pre-paid package you buy. Inquire. My favorite florist is: _____

Purchasing a Cemetery Plot

Your funeral director will help you with this decision. If you already own one, it is located at: _____

Additional Notes

Music

List any music you may want played at your services. _____

_____

_____

Live performance? or CD? _____

Death Certificates

It may be a good idea at this time to consider the number of death certificates your survivors will need. A good *average* would be ten to twelve. You get two for free if you are a Veteran—otherwise only one. Over that, the cost is approximately $10.00 each. The following list will help you decide how many may be necessary. One is needed for each entity, and *your survivors* need one for *their* files.

- Social Security Office
- Veteran's Administration
- Pension Benefits
- Life Insurance Policies—one for each company
- Real Estate Transactions—recording new deed or deeds
- Banks. Each bank may require a certified copy. However, it is our experience that some banks are satisfied to *see* a certified copy, and will merely copy it for their files.
- Safe Deposit Box
- Living Trust
- Credit Card Companies. Some companies have insurance policies built in. Remember to ask.
- Vehicle Titles/Registrations
- Home and automobile insurance companies
- Stocks
- Bonds
- Annuities
- Grazing Permits on State Land or on the Reservations
- Any Court-Mandated Situation in which you may currently be involved
- Don't forget to order one for your records

Additional Notes

Be wise to run the obituary in the paper after funeral services for security reasons

Which newspaper do you prefer?

and then there was one

Information for the Obituary Column

Full Name _____

Parents' Names (use maiden) _____

Date and Place of Marriage _____

Names and Relationships of Survivors

_____

_____

_____

Names of those who preceded you in death _____

_____

_____

Chronological Life History. For example...where you were born; when moved to town; where schooled; years as a veteran; accomplishments

_____

_____

_____

_____

_____

_____

_____

_____

Hobbies Enjoyed _____

Church affiliation and activities _____

Clubs and organizations you are a member of _____

_____

_____

_____

Name and address where charitable contributions can be sent if so desired

_____

_____

_____

5

Additional Notes

Bring this completed form with you to the funeral home

Name		D.O.B.	SS#

Date of Death	Age	If Under One year:
		Months(s)_____ Days_____ Hours_____ Minutes_____

City & State of Birth	Citizen of what Country?

Place of Death: □ Hospital □ Institution	Town/City	State
□ DOA □ Operating Emergency □ In-Patient		

If death occurred at residence, give address

Race: □ White   □ Black   □ American Indian   □ Hispanic

If Hispanic, indicate: □ Mexican   □ Spanish   □ Puerto Rican   □ Cuban   □ Other _____

Was deceased ever in the U.S. Armed Forces? □ Yes   □ No   If Yes, bring copy of your DD214

Was deceased: □ Married   □ Never Married   □ Widowed   □ Divorced

Surviving Spouse	If wife, give maiden name

Usual Occupation	Business or Industry	Education: Highest Grade Completed _____

Was death work-related? □ Yes   □ No   If Yes, contact your local Workers' Compensation Office

Usual Residence (Full Address)	Inside City Limits? □ Yes □ No
	On Reservation? □ Yes □ No

Father's Full Name	Mother's Full Name (Use Maiden Name)

Informant's Information

Print Informant's Name	Relationship to the Deceased

Informant's Signature	Informant's Complete Address

Additional Notes

Quick-Reference Form for the Survivor

DECEASED

Full Name _____

Address _____

Date of Birth _____ Date of Death _____

Decedent's Social Security # _____ Veterans # _____

Driver's License # _____ State of Issuance _____

Maiden Name _____ Mother's Maiden Name _____

SURVIVOR

Full Name _____

Address _____ Phone _____

Date of Birth _____ Social Security # _____

Date & Place of Marriage (if applicable) to decedent _____

Maiden Name _____ Mother's Maiden Name _____

FUNERAL HOME _____ Phone _____

Address _____

Name of Director _____ Contact _____

Location & Date for Viewing _____

Location & Date for Memorial _____

Location & Date for Wake _____

CEMETERY _____ Phone_____

Address _____ Contact _____

Funeral Date _____

Notes: _____

_____

Additional Notes

If your survivors live out of state, they may not know all of your friends. This will help.

and then there was one

Please write, (or call) the following for me.

Name _____

Relationship _____

Address _____

Phone _____

_____

Name _____

Relationship _____

Address _____

Phone _____

_____

Name _____

Relationship _____

Address _____

Phone _____

_____

5

Name _____

Relationship _____

Address _____

Phone _____

_____

Name _____

Relationship _____

Address _____

Phone _____

_____

Name _____

Relationship _____

Address _____

Phone _____

_____

Additional Notes

and then there was one

Letter to My Representatives

To:

Representative Name & Address	Alternate Name & Address
_____	_____
_____	_____
_____	_____
_____	_____

The law allows me to make certain medical and financial decisions as to what I want in the future if I become unable or incapable of making certain decisions for myself. I have completed the following documents and I want you to be my representative for the following purposes:

___ Durable Health Care Power of Attorney with Mental Health Authority
___ General Durable Power of Attorney

I chose two representatives in case one of you is unable to act for me when the time comes. I ask that you accept my selection of you, and will assume you are agreeable if you do not return the enclosed forms and this letter to inform me otherwise.

By selecting you, I want you to make some very important decisions for me about future health care needs if I become unable to make these decisions for myself—even if you do not agree with them. This is a very serious responsibility to accept. You will be my voice to follow through with the medical decisions I have made. Other than what I have indicated in the Powers of Attorney as to my specific directions on certain issues, I am trusting your judgment to make decisions that you believe to be in my best interests.

You will not be financially responsible for paying my health care costs, nor are you liable for complying with my decisions as stated in the Powers of Attorney or in making other health care decisions for me if you act in good faith.

Keep a copy of these documents in a safe place. Read them carefully and feel free to discuss my choices with me at any time. My family, physician, and other representatives will also have a copy. You are hereby authorized to discuss with them the Powers of Attorney, including, as it applies, my medical situation, or any medical concerns about me. Please work with them and help them to act in accordance with my desires and best interests as well. Your support and willingness to help me in this matter is sincerely appreciated.

Signature _____   Date _____

Print your name _____

Although the *sample forms* in the following Section are Arizona-specific, they are included to give you an idea of what these documents should contain.

To find Living Wills and Powers of Attorney to conform to your state, either do a search for Advance Directives on your computer, or go to your local library.

Much caution should be exercised if you are considering preparing your own legal documents. These documents can be very complicated and should be customized to your specific needs to avoid risk of errors.

It is strongly recommended you consult with an attorney.

Advance directives, (Living Will and Powers of Attorney), are relatively inexpensive to have done by a professional, and knowing they have been written up correctly, and customized to your particular needs, is a small price to pay for peace of mind.

Some hospitals will keep your records on file for a nominal fee.
Check into this at your local hospital.

6

PLEASE NOTE

These end-of-life forms do not replace a trusted attorney.
You are advised to seek counsel, as everyone's situation is different, and
these documents should be customized to your specific needs.

Ten Little Mistakes with BIG Consequences

1. I will talk to my family, doctor, lawyer, minister, friend—***later***.
2. I will sign my estate planning documents, put them away, and never read or update them.
3. I won't tell anyone where I keep my important papers or the key to my safe deposit box.
4. I will assume that information that was correct 5 or 10 years ago is still true today.
5. I will make changes to my estate plan by writing in the margins or crossing out and initialing what I do not want anymore.
6. I will assume that my children (and possibly step-children) will get along with one another (and with my spouse) if I become incapacitated or die, regardless of the quality of their relationships with one another today.
7. I will put my children (or others) in positions of trust and authority because I don't want to hurt their feelings.
8. I will decide and tell someone what I want for my funeral or burial—***later***.
9. I won't stay in touch with the people who are my agents under my Powers of Attorney, my Personal Representative or Successor Trustee, and won't update my documents when their, (or my own,) life-circumstances, change.
10. I will assume that my death or incapacity won't change how people in my family relate to one another.

Bonus: *I assume that I will know when I need help and will ask for it and receive what I need and want without considering the* Ten Questions to Ask Myself.

Ten Questions to Ask Myself

1. What part of my independence means the most to me?
2. What makes a day a good day for me?
3. How much time, energy and resources will I (can I) commit, to maintain my independence and be sure my choices are honored?
4. How good am I at accepting help?
5. Who do I trust enough to ask for help?
6. How will I know if I need help?
7. Who knows my wishes about how I want to live if I cannot express myself?
8. Do I know these answers, not just for myself, but also for the people who will rely on me if they become ill or incapacitated?
9. What have I not thought about that may cause my plan to falter or fail?
10. What legal documents have I created to ensure that my choices are honored as I age, if I become ill, incapacitated, and upon my death? How do I know they are adequate and up-to-date?

Reproduced with permission from Susan Robbins, Esq., 15249 N 99th Avenue, Sun City, Arizona, 85351

and then there was one

By Leighton H. Rockafellow
Attorney at Law

We all know we won't live forever. However, most of us put off planning for death, as it is such an unpleasant topic. Just like any other event in life that you prepare for, you need to prepare for the final event. Your survivors will thank you for it and you will spare them additional grief by planning ahead. *If for no other reason than consideration of your family and loved ones—be prepared for death.*

There are legal documents used by all Estate Planners that every person should consider—regardless of their age or monetary circumstances. These documents are:

1. Advance Directives (also known as a Living Will)
2. Durable Health Care Power of Attorney with Mental Health Authority (Terminates at death)
3. General Durable Power of Attorney (Terminates at death)
4. Do Not Resuscitate Order (DNR)

None of these documents become effective until you are incapacitated and no longer in a position to make your own decisions. It is important to have these documents in place before the need arises. Sample forms are included in this workbook, however, they comply with the laws of the State of Arizona. If you are not a resident of the State of Arizona, you are urged to inquire as to their compliance within your State of residence. In addition, for all concerned, hospitals may require different forms and often use their own forms. Please do your homework and look into the specific requirements of your community.

6

1. Advance Directives (Living Will)

Advance Directives are made during your lifetime and specifies your choices regarding health care decisions as your life comes to an end. It usually refers to heroic life-prolonging measurers, such as respirators or other artificial means that keep a person "alive", even though the person is unable to sustain life independent of these devices.

Without Advance Directives, your treating physicians will not allow family members to make life-ending decisions for you. You may be left indefinitely on life-prolonging machines. You should not put your family through the necessity or pain of having to obtain a court order to make these decisions. Think ahead and have your Advance Directives executed while you are still in good health.

When You're Incapacitated...It's Too Late!

There are several reasons to have Powers of Attorney.

Some are...

- if you work in a dangerous/high-risk profession
- if you have become seriously ill or terminal
- if you have young children that may need care in case of your incapacity
- if you travel often
- or if you are simply growing old

Powers of Attorney will make life easier for you and your loved ones.

Caveats about Powers of Attorney

Give much thought about whom you choose...

Make sure they want the job

Make sure of their integrity

Have family meetings so everyone is aware of your choices

Keep in mind...Powers of Attorney terminate upon your death

2. Durable Health Care Power of Attorney with Mental Health Authority (Contingent & Immediate)

A Power of Attorney gives a person the right to make legal decisions for you. A Durable Health Care Power of Attorney with Mental Health Authority gives another person the right to make your health-care-related decisions for you. Under the Federal Health Insurance Portability and Accountability Act, your family, friends or loved ones have no right to have access to your medical records or make any health-care-related decisions on your behalf without a Durable Health Care Power of Attorney. Spare your family the pain of petitioning the court for this right by executing a Durable Health Care Power of Attorney while you are still in good health. All Powers of Attorney terminate upon the death of the principal.

3. General Durable Power of Attorney (Contingent & Immediate)

Like a Power of Attorney, a General Durable Power of Attorney gives another person the right to make legal and financial decisions for you even if you are no longer able to make them for yourself. They contain language stating that the Power of Attorney continues even during periods of your incapacitation or incompetence. All married couples should have reciprocal General Durable Powers of Attorney so that one can make decisions and sign for the other in the absence of the other, even during periods of illness, physical, or mental incapacity. All Powers of Attorney terminate upon the death of the principal.

You can now register your end-of-life documents with the Secretary of State's Office. If you have a computer go to www.azsos.org. Use the drop arrow on Quick Links. Click on Advance Directives. This gives you all the information you need to know to register. They will accept your original documents. If you don't have a computer, call 602.542.6187, or 800.458.5842, or write to them at:
Arizona Secretary of State
Advance Directives
1700 W. Washington – 7th Floor
Phoenix, Arizona 85007

If you do not reside in Arizona, contact your state's Secretary of State's Office and inquire of this service.

4. Do Not Resuscitate Order (DNR)

If you do not wish to be resuscitated, you must have a Do Not Resuscitate Order in recognizable form in the hospital chart. The DNR Order must be printed on **orange paper** and must have a recent photograph of you in the space provided. Provide a copy of this to the treating physician, the hospital, and any ambulance company servicing your area. *This document cannot be registered with the Secretary of State's Office.*

What is Estate Planning?

Writing down what you want to happen in the event of your death or incapacitation regarding:

- Children

- Money

- Healthcare

Reproduced with permission from Jeffrey P. Hall, PLLC, Attorney at Law,
3115 S. Price Road, Chandler, Arizona, 85248

Advance Directives / Living Will

I, _____ of _____ County, State of _____, willfully and voluntarily declare that if my death becomes imminent, my dying shall not be artificially prolonged under the guidelines described below.

Guidelines for the Cessation of Life-Prolonging Procedures

If at any time my medical condition becomes irreversible and terminal, I direct that any life-prolonging procedures shall be withheld or withdrawn.

For this declaration to take effect, my attending physician must determine that there can be no recovery from my terminal condition, and that my death is imminent. Life-prolonging procedures shall include any procedure that would serve only to artificially prolong the dying process. I wish to die naturally, with only the administration of medication or the performance of any medical procedures deemed necessary to provide me with comfort and care or to alleviate pain, even though they may shorten my remaining life.

Statement of My Intent

In the absence of my ability to give directions regarding the use of such life-prolonging procedures, it is my intent that this declaration be honored by my family and physician as the final expression of my legal right to refuse medical or surgical treatment and to accept the consequences of such refusal.

This declaration is made after careful consideration and is in accordance with my strong convictions and beliefs. I want my wishes and directions as expressed in this declaration to be carried out to the extent permitted by law. Insofar as they are not legally enforceable, I hope that my family, my physician, the courts and all others who may be involved in such decision making will regard themselves as morally bound by this declaration.

Additional Notes

Release of Liability

I hereby release and hold harmless any person who, in good faith, terminates life-sustaining procedures in accordance with the guidelines in this declaration.

I understand the full import of this declaration, and I am emotionally and mentally competent to make this declaration.

Dated _____

_____
Testator (Your signature or mark)

_____
Print your name

_____
Print name of Witness #1

_____
Signature of Witness #1

Address

_____

_____

_____
Print name of Witness #2

_____
Signature of Witness #2

Address

_____

_____

6

Additional Notes

and then there was one

STATE OF _____)

                                          : §

COUNTY OF _____)

I, _____ , the Testator, in the presence of the witnesses, _____ and _____ signed the instrument as his Living Will, that he signed, and that each of the witnesses, in the presence of the Testator and in the presence of each other, signed the Living Will as a witness.

_____

Testator

_____

Witness

_____

Witness

Subscribed and sworn before me by _____

the Testator, and by _____ and _____

the witnesses, on _____ .

_____

Notary Public

My commission expires

_____

and then there was one

Additional Notes

and then there was one

Durable Health Care Power of Attorney
with Mental Health Authority

I,_____ do hereby designate and appoint
_____ as my Agent to make health care decisions for me as
authorized in this document. In the event the designated appointee cannot act as my agent, I
designate and appoint _____ to serve as my agent.

1. **GENERAL STATEMENT OF AUTHORITY GRANTED:**
    If I no longer have the capacity to make health care decisions for myself, I hereby
    grant to my agent full power and authority to make health care decisions for me to
    the same extent that I could make such decisions for myself if I had the capacity
    to do so. My incapacity to make health care decisions for myself shall be certified
    in writing by my treating physician. In exercising this authority, I request my agent
    to make health care decisions that are consistent with my desires as stated in this
    document or which I have otherwise made known to my agent. My agent may also
    make health care decisions about which I have not stated my desires.

2. **STATEMENT OF DESIRES, SPECIAL PROVISIONS, AND LIMITATIONS.**
    I do not fear death itself as much as the indignities of deterioration, dependence
    and hopeless pain. I request that my agent refuse or require discontinuance of any
    medical treatment, which will only prolong the process of dying or my irreversible
    coma. In such circumstances, I request that my agent consent to and arrange for
    the administration of drugs or medical procedures to alleviate my pain even though
    such drugs or procedures may lead to permanent physical damage or addiction or
    may hasten the moment of my death.

3. **INSPECTION AND DISCLOSURE OF INFORMATION RELATING TO MY
    PHYSICAL OR MENTAL HEALTH; SIGNING DOCUMENTS; CONSENTS; AND
    RELEASES:**

    My agent has the power and authority to:
    Obtain medical and health care records and any other information regarding my:

    a.) Physical or mental health;
    b.) Execute on my behalf any releases or other documents that may be required in
        order to obtain such information;
    c.) Consent to the disclosure of such information to others;
    d.) Execute any document necessary to implement the health care decisions made
        by my agent, including but not limited to hospital and nursing home admission
        agreements and consent forms;
    e.) Execute any waiver or release from liability that my agent determines to be
        appropriate;
    f.) Execute any document necessary to obtain or effect reimbursement or payment
        for services rendered to me.
    g.) Admit me, upon the recommendation by a psychiatrist or psychologist who has
        examined me, to a level-one behavioral health facility licensed by the State
        Department of Health, for evaluation and treatment.

1 of 3.

Additional Notes

4. DURATION:

This Power of Attorney shall be effective until I expressly revoke it, however, it shall not be revocable or otherwise affected by my subsequent disability or incapacity nor shall it be revocable by a guardian. I hereby release all persons from any liability arising from their reliance on this Power of Attorney if they have no actual knowledge that I have revoked it. To the fullest extent possible, I release my agent from all liability to me, my estate, and any other person for any actions taken hereunder in good faith.

5. PRIOR DESIGNATIONS REVOKED:

If applicable, I revoke my prior Health Care Power of Attorney.

_____ By initialing here, I specifically consent to giving my agent the power to admit me to an in-patient or partial psychiatric hospitalization program if ordered by my physician.

_____ By initialing here, this Health Care Directive including Mental Health Care Power of Attorney, may not be revoked if I am incapacitated.

I intend for my Agent to be treated as I would be with respect to my rights regarding the use and disclosure of my individually identifiable health information or other medical records. This release authority applies to any information governed by the Health Insurance Portability and Accountability Act of 1996 (aka HIPAA), 42 U.S.C. § 1320(d) and 45 C.F.R. §§ 160-164 and applies even if that person has not yet been appointed as Agent but is next in line to become Agent.

Initial ONE of the following two choices. This will determine when your Power of Attorney becomes effective. Cross through the choice you have not selected.

_____ **THESE HEALTH CARE POWERS ARE EFFECTIVE IMMEDIATELY UPON EXECUTION.**

This Power of Attorney is effective immediately upon my signing this document. When this document is executed, I intend for my Agent to be treated as I would be with respect to my rights regarding the use and disclosure of my individually identifiable health information or other medical records, including any written opinion relating to my mental or physical illness, injury, disability or incapacity. Pursuant to HIPAA, I authorize any covered health care provider, insurance company, or any health care information clearinghouse that has provided or paid for services to me or is seeking payment for such services, to release to my Agent, without restriction, all of my individually identifiable health information and medical records regarding past, present or future medical or mental health conditions, including HIV/AIDS, STDs, mental illness and drug or alcohol abuse. The authority given to my Agent shall supersede any prior agreement that I have made with my health care providers to restrict access to or disclosure of my individually identifiable health information. This authority has no expiration date, and shall expire only upon written revocation by me with actual notice to the health care provider.

and then there was one

181

Additional Notes

and then there was one

THESE HEALTH CARE POWERS ARE CONTINGENT ONLY UPON THE DISABILITY OF THE PRINCIPAL.

This Power of Attorney is effective only upon my inability to make or communicate health care decisions, as determined by, in writing, my physician of record (treating physician), or, in an emergency, by a physician who has examined and treated me within thirty (30) days of the time such certification of disability is needed. Upon such determination, I intend for my Agent to be treated as I would be with respect to my rights regarding the use and disclosure of my individually identifiable health information or other medical records, including any written opinion relating to my mental or physical illness, injury, disability or incapacity. Pursuant to HIPAA, I authorize any covered health care provider, insurance company, or any health care information clearinghouse that has provided or paid for services to me or is seeking payment for such services, to release to my Agent, without restriction, all of my individually identifiable health information and medical records regarding past, present or future medical or mental health conditions, including HIV/AIDS, STDs, mental illness and drug or alcohol abuse. The authority given to my Agent shall supersede any prior agreement that I have made with my health care providers to restrict access to or disclosure of my individually identifiable health information. This authority has no expiration date, and shall expire only upon written revocation by me with actual notice to the health care provider. However, at such time as any physician as described above determines that I am again able to make decisions regarding my own health care, my wishes shall supersede those of any of my agents herein.

DATED THIS _____ day of _____, 20_____.

_____

Principal

We declare that we know the person who signed this document as principal, that the principal signed in our presence; that the principal appears to be of sound mind and under no duress, fraud or undue influence, and that we are not persons appointed as agents by this document.

_____   _____

Witness   Witness

STATE OF _____)

                                                 : §

COUNTY OF _____)

     PERSONALLY CAME before me this _____ day of_____, 20 _____, the above-named _____ to me known to be the person described in and who executed the foregoing instrument and acknowledged the same as his free act and deed.

_____

Notary

My commission expires:

_____

and then there was one   183

Additional Notes

and then there was one

General Durable Power of Attorney

TO ALL PERSONS, be it known that I, _____, of _____ County, State of _____, the undersigned Grantor, do hereby make and grant a General Durable Power of Attorney to _____ of _____ County, State of _____, and do thereupon constitute and appoint said individual as my Attorney-in-Fact/Agent.

My Attorney-in-Fact/Agent shall act in my name, place and stead in any way which I myself could do, if I were personally present, with respect to the following matters, to the extent that I am permitted by law to act through an agent:

Grantor MUST initial the space to designate authorization for the itemized transaction(s).

_____ Real Estate transactions   _____ Banking transactions
_____ Tangible personal property transactions   _____ Bond, share and commodity transactions
_____ Business Operating transactions   _____ Insurance transactions
_____ Claims and Litigation   _____ Personal relationships & affairs
_____ Benefits from military service   _____ Records, reports & statements
_____ Access to safe deposit boxes   _____ *Authorize medical & surgical procedures
                                               (*Pennsylvania only)

_____ Gifts to charities & individuals other than Attorney-in-Fact/Agent
_____ Full and unqualified authority to my Attorney-in-Fact/Agent to delegate any or all of the foregoing powers or persons whom my Attorney-in-Fact/Agent shall select.
_____ All other matters
_____ This Power of Attorney shall not be affected by the subsequent disability or incompetence of the Grantor.

My Attorney-in-Fact/Agent hereby accepts this appointment subject to its terms and agrees to act and perform in said fiduciary capacity consistent with my best interests as he/she in his/her best discretion deems advisable, and I affirm and ratify all acts so undertaken.

To induce any third party to act hereunder, I hereby agree that any third party receiving a duly executed copy or facsimile of this instrument may act hereunder, and that revocation or termination hereof shall be ineffective as to such third party unless and until actual notice or knowledge of such revocation or termination shall have been received by such third party, and I for myself and for my heirs, executors, legal representatives and assigns, hereby agree to indemnify and hold harmless any such third party from and against any and all claims that may arise against such third party by reason of such third party having relied on the provisions of this instrument.

I intend for my Agent to be treated as I would be with respect to my rights regarding the use and disclosure of my individually identifiable health information or other medical records. This release authority applies to any information governed by the Health Insurance Portability and Accountability Act of 1996 (aka HIPAA), 42 U.S.C.§ 1320d and 45 C.F.R. §§ 160-164 and applies even if that person has not yet been appointed as Agent but is next in line to become Agent.

Initial ONE of the following two choices. This will determine when your Power of Attorney becomes effective. Cross through the choice you have not selected.

_____   **THESE GENERAL DURABLE FINANCIAL POWERS ARE EFFECTIVE IMMEDIATELY.**

The preceding Powers granted by Principal to Agent shall become effective upon the Principal's signature and acknowledgment below. Powers granted to Agent by Principal shall not thereafter be affected by the Principal's disability, incapacity, or incompetency, A.R.S. §§ 14-5501, 14-5502, and shall not be affected by the lapse of time.

This General Power of Attorney may be revoked by the Principal giving actual written notice to anyone dealing with the Attorney-in-Fact or by recording a Revocation of this Power of Attorney with the County Recorder of said County, State of _____. A third party is entitled to rely upon this Power of Attorney until notified in writing that it has been revoked or until notified in writing of the death of the Principal.

Additional Notes

and then there was one

_____ THESE GENERAL DURABLE FINANCIAL POWERS ARE CONTINGENT ONLY UPON THE PRINCIPAL'S DISABILITY AS DEFINED BELOW.

The preceding powers granted by Principal to Agent shall become effective only upon the Principal's incapacity or incompetency, as certified in writing by the Principal's attending physician, if available, or any licensed health care provider who has examined or treated the Principal, and said powers shall not thereafter be affected by the Principal's disability, incapacity, or incompetency, A.R.S. §§ 14-5501, 14-5502, and shall not be affected by the lapse of time.

This General Power of Attorney may be revoked by the Principal giving actual written notice to anyone dealing with the Attorney-in-Fact or by recording a Revocation of this Power of Attorney with the County Recorder of Maricopa County, Arizona. A third party is entitled to rely upon this Power of Attorney until notified in writing that it has been revoked or until notified in writing of the death of the Principal.

If, at any time, either or both of my Co-Agents have questions about my ability to make or communicate health care decisions, my Agents are authorized to obtain any information, including my individually identifiable health information or other medical records governed by the Health Insurance Portability and Accountability Act of 1996 ("HIPAA"), 42 USC 1320(d) and 45 CFR 160-164, and also including any written opinion relating to my mental or physical illness, injury, disability or incapacity, in order to resolve the question.

Signed under seal this _____ day of _____, 20 _____

_____   _____
Grantor   Attorney-in-Fact/Agent

_____   _____
Witness   Witness

STATE OF _____)
                               : §
COUNTY OF _____)

    PERSONALLY CAME before me this _____ day of _____ , 20 _____, the above-named _____ to me known to be the person described in and who executed the foregoing instrument and acknowledged the same as his free act and deed.

WITNESS my hand and official seal.

                                      _____
                                        Notary

My commission expires_____

6

Additional Notes

DO NOT RESUSCITATE ORDER (DNR)

PRE-HOSPITAL MEDICAL CARE DIRECTIVE

In the event of cardiac or respiratory arrest, I refuse any resuscitation measures including cardiac compression, endotracheal intubation and other advanced airway management, artificial ventilation, defibrillation, administration of advanced cardiac life support drugs and related emergency medical procedures.

WARNING! DO NOT SIGN UNLESS YOU ARE TERMINAL AND/OR NO LONGER WANT MEDICAL INTERVENTION

Patient _____ Date _____
signature or mark

I was present when this form was signed or marked by the patient. Patient appeared to be of sound mind and free from duress.

Signature of Witness _____ Date _____

Your doctor's name _____ Phone _____

I have explained this form and its consequences to the signer/patient, and obtained assurance that the signer understands that death may result from any refused care listed above.

Signature of licensed health care provider_____ Date _____

Hospice program (if any) _____ Phone _____
Name of Hospice personnel _____

This form is on ORANGE CARDSTOCK

6

Attach <u>recent</u> photo of yourself here

AND

Provide required information
to the right ▶

Patient Information

Date of Birth_____

Eye Color_____

Hair Color_____

Male ( )   Female ( )

Race _____

*A*nother organization recently brought to my attention is:

Science Care
21410 N. 19th Ave., Suite 126
Phoenix, AZ 85027
1.800.417.3747
info@sciencecare.com
www.sciencecare.com

Science Care is a whole body donation program for medical research and education. They link people who want to donate their body to science with medical researchers and educators who are using human tissue to improve healthcare for future generations. An individual can either join the donor registry before they pass away or their next of kin can provide consent at the time of passing. There is no cost to the donation program, which includes transportation, cremation, filing of the death certificate, and return of the cremated remains in 3-5 weeks. Science Care is the first program in the country to be accredited by the American Association of Tissue Banks. They are available 24/7 by email, phone, or online.

Donors support projects such as cancer research through the National Cancer Institute, research on heart disease and Alzheimer's, as well as training doctors on the latest medical devices and techniques. The family receives a letter after donation detailing those projects, and a tree is planted in honor of the donor at the one-year donation anniversary through the Arbor Day Foundation.

If you die out of the country, you no longer qualify for the program.

Yet another decision to make is whether or not to donate your whole body, or some of the organs, bones, skin, etc. To help you with this decision, you may contact the following organizations:

Research for Life
131 S. Weber Drive
Chandler, Az.   85226
480.940.1310
800.229.3244
www.researchforlifeaz.org

Research for Life is a whole body donation organization benefiting medical research and education. There is no cost to be a donor with Research for Life. They provide donor families with personal, compassionate, service they deserve. The cremains are returned to the survivors in approximately three to four weeks. It's easy to register, and once qualified into their program, acceptance of the body is guaranteed, even if the donor's health history has changed. Your loved one will still be cremated and returned to you. *If you are pre-registered and die out of state, you are still covered. If you die out of the country, you are not covered.*

Call for a brochure and additional information. Their office hours are Monday through Friday, 9 to 5. A caring staff member answers after-hours calls 24 hours a day, seven days a week.

6

If you wish to donate your organs and tissue upon your death, you must register with Donor Network of Arizona (DNA), the state's only organ procurement organization and tissue/eye recovery organization.

Donor Network of Arizona
201 W. Coolidge,
Phoenix, AZ   85013
602.222.2200
800.94 DONOR (800.943.6667)
www.donatelifeaz.org

DNA is a federally designated, nonprofit organization that serves five organ transplant centers in Arizona with the combined capacity to perform heart, lung, kidney, pancreas and liver transplants. When a person is dead or near death, hospitals call DNA. The patient's medical condition and history is then reviewed to determine if the patient qualifies to become a donor. There is no cost to becoming a donor. The family bears the expense of any funeral arrangements. Your generous decision to donate saves lives. *If you die out of state or out of the country, you will be a donor for that state or country.*

Additional Notes

List below those you gave a copy to, and other places you put them.

and then there was one

*F*ollowing is a form that will be helpful in emergency situations. It is fashioned after other forms, but includes additional information regarding end-of-life documents and the like. You may wish to keep a copy on your refrigerator, on the visor in your vehicle(s), and hand one out to responsible family members, neighbors, or Personal Representative.

Emergency Information

Name: _____
Age: _____ D.O.B.:_____
Weight: _____

Medical Problems	Medication(s)	Dosage	Frequency

Known Food and Drug Allergies					

Health Insurance Company: _____ Member Number: _____
Primary Care Physician: _____ Phone: _____
SPECIALIST: _____ Phone: _____

Check what applies:

( ) I have Advance Directives (also known as a Living Will)
( ) I have a Durable Health Care Power of Attorney with Mental Health Authority
( ) I have a General Durable Power of Attorney
( ) I have a Last Will and Testament
( ) I have a Living Trust
( ) I have a DO NOT RESUSCITATE ORDER
( ) I am an organ donor
Documents located at: _____
( ) I am Registered with Secretary of State www.azsos.org
Religion: _____ Contact: _____

Tip: Copy on bright colored paper first. Cut along dotted lines. Fill in the blanks.
Then make as many copies as you need. Don't forget your doctor.

and then there was one

Additional Notes

Once you have visited your trust attorney and/or estate planner and secured your medical directive documents, complete the following Wallet-Sized Notice for yourself and/or loved one. (You may want to copy on bright colored paper to locate easier). Then...

- Cut along outside edge.
- Write your name and date on the top half, initial appropriate boxes, then add the name(s) and phone number(s) of your emergency contacts on the bottom half.
- Check whether or not you are *"registered with the Secretary of State's Office"*. See **Page 171**.
- Fold in half, laminate and keep it in your wallet with your driver's license and insurance cards.

Law enforcement and medical personnel will then know that you have these completed health care documents. It is a good idea to keep copies of the forms that you designate on this Notice in a waterproof bag in the glove compartment of your vehicle, a safe place in your home, in the hands of your designated POA, and anywhere or anyone else you deem necessary.

NOTICE: In Case of Accident or Other Emergency:

Name ______________________

Date ______________________

I have signed the following forms:
Put a check mark (✓) & initial next to what applies:

___ Advance Directives (formerly Living Will)
___ Durable Health Care Power of Attorney with Mental Health Authority
___ General Durable Power of Attorney
___ Anatomical Gift
___ Do Not Resuscitate Order (DNR)

Fold Here ▶ — — — — — — — — — — —

Emergency Contact

Name:______________________

Phone:______________________

Alternate:

Name ______________________

Phone:______________________

( ) I am... ( ) I am not...
registered with the Secretary of State's Office

6

Additional Notes

It is strongly suggested by estate planners, that you make a list of your Tangible Personal Property. Circulate this list amongst the recipients. They can then make their choices during happy times, and not under the duress that a death will create. Many family arguments can then be averted.

and then there was one

By Leighton H. Rockafellow
Attorney at Law

**This document should be kept with your Will,
and is only valid when used in conjunction with a Will**

*T*he following are instructions for using the Memorandum for Distribution of Tangible
Personal Property on **Page 199**.

1. The Memorandum should not include items already specifically disposed of by
   you, by your Will, or by your Trust.

2. The use of such a Memorandum is not intended to apply to the disposition of
   money, promissory notes, or other evidences of indebtedness, documents of
   title, securities or any property used in a trade or business.

3. The Memorandum should be dated and signed by you.

4. You should clearly describe each item so that it can be easily identified and will
   not be confused with another similar item.

5. The item number of the description should match the item number of the
   recipient.

6. Each page of your Memorandum should be signed and dated and should be
   witnessed by someone who is neither a relative nor a recipient.

7. Each designated recipient should be identified by his or her proper name and
   relationship to you. The address of the recipient should be added if he or she
   does not live in the same household as you.

8. You may change the recipients or property designated in the Memorandum
   from time-to-time, or revise or revoke the entire Memorandum. Changes
   should be made only by using a blank copy of this Memorandum, or creating
   a new Memorandum patterned after this form. The old Memorandum should
   be destroyed. Changes should *never* be made by striking through an item,
   or altering anything on the Memorandum, after it has been executed. Such
   changes could affect the validity of the entire Memorandum, since it might not
   be possible at a later time to determine whether you or someone else made the
   changes.

9. You may make copies of this completed Memorandum for your convenience
   and that of your recipients.

6

Photograph(s) of your gift(s)

and then there was one

Pursuant to A.R.S. §14-2513, and in conjunction with my Will, dated _____, I hereby request my Personal Representative to distribute the following items of non-business tangible personal property as follows:

Description of Tangible Personal Property	Recipient of Tangible Personal Property

If a recipient of a particular item of non-business personal property does not survive me, such item shall be disposed of as though it had not been listed in this Memorandum.

_____ _____
Date *Signature*

6

Additional Notes

♥ Our Pets Grieve Too ♥

Visit your local library and hospice, or do an Internet search on the subject.

You'll be glad you did.

and then there was one

Your pets and other animals should not be overlooked. Someone will have to provide for them in your absence. Even if you merely go on vacation, this information will be helpful to their caretaker. Make as many copies as you need. Each pet should have their own record. Keep **their** records in a safe place too.

Name of Pet _____ Type of Pet _____

Age _____ DOB _____ Sex _____

Breed _____ Color & Markings _____

Tag Number _____

Veterinarian _____ Address _____

Phone _____

Emergency # _____

Pet Insurance? ( ) Yes ( ) No Name of Company _____

Policy Number _____ Phone _____

List Rx Drugs currently administered

_____

Naturopathic remedies

_____

Notes _____

_____

6

Owner Information	Caretaker Information
Name _____	Name _____
Address _____	Address _____
Phone _____	Phone _____

I, _____ , owner of the above pet, authorize _____

to act on my behalf if there is an emergency.

_____ _____
Date *Signature*

1. Copy the form below on bright neon paper, (as many as you need),
2. Cut along the outside edge of the dashed line,
3. Fill in the blanks,
4. Laminate and post in a front window or on your front door.

Emergency crews will then know that you have pets or other animals that need help.

In case of an emergency
PLEASE RESCUE MY PET

_____   _____
Name and Type of Pet   **Date**

My Cell #: _____

Veterinarian: _____

Phone: _____

_____
Relative / Friend, Name & Phone Number

Notes to Crew:_____
                               Coloring, age, biter, illnesses, etc.

_____

and then there was one

In Case your Pet has to be Put to Rest

As hurtful as it is, there is yet another reality we may have to face one day. As for a loved one who is human, making arrangements for a beloved pet can be very traumatic at the time of death. It's hard when you're in the moment to deal with paperwork. Doing so ahead of time will free you of *that* part of the process.

The following information was provided to me from local animal hospitals. This information is necessary when it comes time. Fill out what you can when you are able. I know this is hard to do or even think about.

I certify that I am the owner (or authorized agent for the owner) of the pet described in the attached,(use form on opposite page) and that to the best of my knowledge, this animal has not...

() bitten any person during the previous 15 days,
() been exposed to rabies, and
() is current on its rabies vaccination.

I give Dr. _____ and his agents at _____
                                                                    Name of Business

the complete authority to euthanize the above-described animal and forever release the

said Doctor and his agents from all liability for euthanizing the said animal.

Upon euthanizing, this animal should be: ( ) Returned to owner for burial
                                           ( ) Cremated
                                           ( ) Cremated with ashes returned to owner
                                           ( ) Other: _____

Owner: _____   Address: _____
       Sign your name

                                  _____

Phone: _____

Cell Phone: _____

**Your vet's office may have their own form that you must sign.
Check with their office to see if they will accept this.**

Additional Notes

SECTION SEVEN

Instructions for Form Letters—Pages 207-209

Within these pages, you are given specific instructions as to how to fill in the blanks on the form letters provided within this section.

Form Letters #1 through #8—Pages 211-225

These form letters were designed to help you conduct your business matters in an efficient manner during a time when it is difficult to do. Your friend can help you by using these simplified forms so you don't have to try to think of what to say. The letters are written for you. Simply fill in the applicable blanks.

Sample Letters Announcing the Death of Your Loved One—Page 227

Oftentimes doctors, other professionals, or long-lost friends, will not be aware of the passing of your loved one. It would be a courtesy to them and yourself, to inform them of the death so any appointments made ahead of time may be cancelled. If you have extras, include a memorial card supplied by the funeral home.

Sample Thank You Note—Page 227

It's difficult to manage your daily life, and even more difficult at times to express words of thanks to the many people that will help you during this traumatic time in your life. I include in this Section, a sample that you could use as a guideline for your Thank You notes.

7

Additional Notes

and then there was one

Form Letter #1 to your Mortgage Company or Landlord—Page 211

- Date
- Name and Address of your mortgage company or landlord
- Your account number
- The dollar amount you are enclosing
- Include payment coupon if your mortgage company provides these
- If your mortgage company allows you to pay by credit card, complete the portion provided for this method
- Sign in space provided and complete your return-mail information as outlined in the spaces under your signature
- **Make a copy of the completed letter, and mail**

Form Letter #2 for Insurance Companies—Page 213

- Date
- Name and Address of insurance company
- Fill in the blanks in the "RE:" portion
- Fill in the blank in the body of the letter
- Sign and supply return address information
- They may require a copy of the decedent's death certificate. When you talk to them on the phone, inquire if this is necessary at this time
- **Make a copy of the completed letter and mail**

Form Letter #3 for the Dept. of Veterans Affairs (was decedent a veteran?)—Page 215

- Date
- Fill in the blanks in the "RE:" portion
- Sign in space provided and complete your return-mail information as outlined in the spaces under your signature
- They may require a copy of the decedent's death certificate. When you talk to them on the phone, inquire if this is necessary at this time
- **Make a copy of the completed letter, and mail**

Form Letter #4 —Page 217: Letter in <u>addition</u> to Form #3 (if decedent was a veteran)

Additional Notes

Form Letter #5 is a sample Hardship Letter to Creditors—Page 219

Use the style of this letter if paying your bills will create a financial hardship for you. Write an original letter instead of copying this form and filling in the blanks. Remember to send a 'Thank-You' note if they respond favorably to your request, or if they make other efforts or suggestions on your behalf that will help you.

Form Letter #6 to report death to Credit Card Companies—Page 221

Use this letter as a follow-up to your phone call in which you cancelled or changed over to your name only, credit card companies that you previously notified of the death. They may require a copy of the decedent's death certificate. When you talk to them on the phone, inquire if this is necessary.

Form Letter #7 for Passport Issuing Agency—Page 223

Use this letter to notify the passport issuing office of the death of the decedent. Locate the phone number for passport applications in the blue pages of your phone book. They will give you the address to mail the information to. Once you have the address of the issuing agency, complete this form letter, and include a copy of that portion of the passport which shows the passport number, and photo of the decedent. Also include a copy of the death certificate.

Form Letter #8 for Business Entities—Page 225

Use this letter to reiterate notification of death and substance of conversations you had with business entities (other than those listed above).

**Remember to keep copies
of your completed form letters for your records**

Additional Notes

Keep copies of your completed letters and make notes of conversations

and then there was one

Date _____

Mortgage Company or Landlord and Address

_____

_____

_____

_____

RE: Account Number _____

To Whom it May Concern:

Please apply the enclosed check in the amount of $ _____ to the above account number.

Thank you.

Sincerely,

_____
Your Signature

Print Your Name _____

Address _____

City, State, Zip Code _____

Phone #(s) _____

E-mail Address _____

Enclosures--Check Number _____ & Payment Coupon (if supplied)

If your landlord / lender permits you to pay with a credit card, complete the following:

Type of card: ( ) Visa   ( ) Mastercard   ( ) Discover   ( ) American Express

Card Number:_____   Name on Card:_____

Expiration Date:_____   Signature:_____

Additional Notes

Keep copies of your completed letters and make notes of conversations

and then there was one

Date _____

Insurance Company name and address

_____

_____

_____

_____

RE: Name of Deceased_____

Social Security #_____

Date of Death _____

Policy Number _____

To Whom It May Concern:

Please send instructions and all necessary forms to file a claim for life insurance benefits entitled to the undersigned as beneficiary due to the death of my late _____ (relationship).

Respectfully submitted,

_____
Beneficiary's Signature

Print Your Name _____

Address _____

City, State, Zip Code _____

Phone #(s) _____

E-mail Address _____

Additional Notes

Keep copies of your completed letters and make notes of conversations

and then there was one

Date _____

Department of Veterans Affairs
Regional Office and Insurance Center
Wissahickon Avenue and Manheim Street
P.O. Box 7208
Philadelphia, PA   19101

RE: Name of Deceased _____

Social Security # _____

Military Branch _____ Dates of Service _____

Date of Death _____

To Whom It May Concern:

Please be advised of the death of the above-mentioned Veteran. I wish to inquire as to any benefits for which I may be eligible.

Accordingly, please send the information, instructions, and/or forms necessary to effectuate the filing for same.

Respectfully,

_____
Beneficiary's Signature

Print Your Name _____

Address _____

City, State, Zip Code _____

Phone #(s) _____

E-mail Address _____

Additional Notes

Keep copies of your completed letters and make notes of conversations

and then there was one

Date _____

Office of Servicemen's Group Life Insurance (OSGLI)
290 W. Mt. Pleasant Avenue
Livingston, NJ 07039-2747

RE: Name of Deceased _____

Social Security # _____

Military Branch _____ Dates of Service _____

Date of Death _____

To Whom It May Concern:

Please be advised of the death of the above-mentioned Veteran. I wish to inquire as to any benefits for which I may be eligible.

Accordingly, please send any information, instructions, or forms necessary to effectuate the filing for same.

Respectfully,

_____
Beneficiary's Signature

Print Your Name _____

Address _____

City, State, Zip Code _____

Phone #(s) _____

E-mail Address _____

Additional Notes

Keep copies of your completed letters and make notes of conversations

From _____
_____
_____
Phone _____

Date _____

TO :

_____
_____
_____
_____

RE: Account Number _____

Balance Due $ _____

To Whom It May Concern:

Please forgive my delay in responding to your past-due notices.

This is in regard to the balance due on this account.

My_____(state relationship), died suddenly on _____. Please consider waiving this balance due. The estate is insolvent, and there are insufficient funds to pay this balance.

We have been customers since _____, and our prior payment history has been exemplary.

Your consideration and prompt reply will be appreciated.

Respectfully,

_____
Sign your name

Additional Notes

Keep copies of your completed letters and make notes of conversations

and then there was one

Date _____

Credit Card Company name and address

_____

_____

_____

_____

    RE: Name of Deceased _____

           Social Security #_____

           Date of Death _____

           Credit Card #_____

To Whom It May Concern:

This letter will confirm our phone conversation of _____. To reiterate, you were notified of the death of my_____ (state relationship). I make request of you to cancel the above credit card at your earliest convenience. Enclosed you will find a photocopy of the death certificate. If you require additional information, please feel free to contact me.

Respectfully submitted,

_____

Survivor's Signature

Print Your Name _____

Address _____

City, State, Zip Code _____

Phone #(s) _____

E-mail Address _____

Additional Notes

Keep copies of your completed letters and make notes of conversations

and then there was one

Date _____

Passport issuing agency and address

_____

_____

_____

_____

    RE: Name of Deceased_____

             Social Security # _____

             Date of Birth _____

             Date of Death _____

             Passport Number _____

To Whom It May Concern:

Please be advised of the death of my _____ (state relationship). Enclosed you will find a photocopy of the death certificate, as well as a copy of that portion of the passport which includes the photo and passport number. If you require additional information, please feel free to contact me.

Respectfully submitted,

_____

Survivor's Signature

Print Your Name _____

Address _____

City, State, Zip Code _____

Phone #(s) _____

E-mail Address _____

Additional Notes

Keep copies of your completed letters and make notes of conversations

Date _____

Business entity name and address

_____

_____

_____

_____

RE: Name of Deceased _____

Social Security # _____

Date of Death _____

Account/Reference # _____

To Whom It May Concern:

This letter will confirm our phone conversation of _____. To reiterate, you were notified of the death of my _____ (state relationship). Enclosed you will find a photocopy of the death certificate. In addition, we discussed the following:

If you require additional information, please feel free to contact me.

Respectfully submitted,

_____

Survivor's Signature

Print Your Name _____

Address _____

City, State, Zip Code _____

Phone #(s) _____

E-mail Address _____

People You Have Written

*I*t is very difficult to manage your daily life, and also difficult at times to express words of thanks to the many people that helped you during this time. Following are some sample notes just to get you started. Embellish as you feel, and remember, *there is no rush to get this done.* People understand. Remember too—it's all right to have a friend help you.

Sample Announcement Letter

Oftentimes, doctors, and other professionals, will not be aware of the passing of your loved one. It would be a courtesy to them (and yourself), to inform them of the death so any appointments made ahead of time may be canceled. If you have extras, include a memorial card supplied by the funeral home.

Dear _____

A brief note to inform you of the passing of _____ Please cancel any appointments he/she may have had with your office. I enclose a copy of the memorial card for your records.

Sincerely,

OR maybe not so formal...

Please make a note in your file that _____ passed away on _____ . I enclose a copy of the memorial card for your records. Please cancel any pending appointments.

Sincerely,

Sample Thank You Note

Dear _____

Thank you for your loving kindness, support, and condolences after _____ passed away. As I'm sure you can imagine, (or know), it's been a very difficult and trying time. The transition is overwhelming, but please know how much your thoughtfulness has meant to me.

Thank you.

♥ Remember to send notes to friends you have been out of touch with. ♥

Additional Notes

SECTION EIGHT

8

"The bitterest tears shed over graves are for words left unsaid and deeds left undone."
—Harriet Beecher Stowe

and then there was one

Additional Notes

As the trusted friend who wants to help the survivor, try to remind family, friends, and neighbors that now is not the time to air dirty laundry, have fights, or prey upon the survivor like a vulture over road kill. Much shame should be visited on anyone who can't behave during this time. We have all heard the horror stories—absolutely unbelievable horror stories. Do your best to prevent the survivor from being victimized on top of everything else they have had to endure. Put yourself in their shoes, and try to imagine the impact of such an adjustment in one's lifestyle. They need to be protected. It's a time to be kind to one another. The following are some suggestions to assist the bereaved.

- ♥ Offer to house sit and/or baby sit during visitations and/or funeral.
- ♥ Notify friends who may not yet be aware of the death.
- ♥ Be a quiet and patient listener.
- ♥ Help with their bookkeeping and other financial matters. This can be overwhelming.
- ♥ Start many of your sentences with… "When you feel up to it, let's…"
    - …go out for coffee or dinner or a movie.
    - …get together for a walk or sport they may be interested in.
    - …go grocery shopping together.
    - …have a spa day or just a massage.
- ♥ Prepare a meal or dessert.
- ♥ Do house cleaning or wash dishes. If you see something that needs to be done—just do it.
- ♥ Do laundry if you see it piling up.
- ♥ Take out the trash or recyclables.
- ♥ Do yard work, or shovel snow.
- ♥ Check to see if there is gas in their car.
- ♥ Address 'Thank-you' notes.
- ♥ Be cognizant of what they may or may not eat or drink.
- ♥ Give them a call or 'drop in' in the evening. This is the loneliest time of day.
- ♥ If you can spare it, and if the survivor needs it, offer money to help.
- ♥ Encourage the survivor to journal. Oftentimes, writing is helpful in the healing process.

Try to offer to do several of these things on a regular basis as time passes. The individual may not accept on your first, second, or even third offer, but persevere. It will help them understand that you are sincere about your offer of assistance and your concern for their welfare. Perhaps helping the bereaved do these things may be a motivating factor for them, as sometimes the simplest of chores can be overwhelming. You will know when it's time to start pulling away, and the time has come when your friend can take care of some of the daily chores on his or her own. Doing so may be therapeutic for them.

When a year has passed, write the widowed a special note on the anniversary of their spouse's death. You may also want to do the same on their wedding anniversary date. They will be grateful for your note of support that says: ♥ *someone else remembers* ♥

8

Additional Notes

Twelve Creeds to Live by During Grief

As a close friend of the survivor, stay attentive to their progress towards healing. Present the following words of encouragement when you feel he or she will be most receptive.

- ♥ I will allow myself time to grieve, for every day offers healing.

- ♥ Healing is a slow process; and most emotions cannot be controlled.

- ♥ Grief affects me emotionally, physically, sexually and spiritually.

- ♥ I will grieve as long as I need to; my grief will pass.

- ♥ Things seldom happen the way I imagine or think they will occur.

- ♥ Thinking about all the 'if only's' is non-productive.

- ♥ I will take care of myself and be attentive to my needs.

- ♥ Grieving does not mean letting go of the one I loved.

- ♥ Everyone experiences loss; I will probably never forget. I will learn how to live with my loss.

- ♥ In grieving the death of my loved one, I grieve other losses as well.

- ♥ When I repress my feelings I give them power. When I embrace them, I gain strength.

- ♥ I have the ability and inner resources to deal with my pain and survive my loss.

8

Additional Notes

*T*he death of a loved one is a life-altering experience. Unless you've 'been there and done that' yourself, it is impossible to comprehend what it feels like. We want to hear words like…*I'm so sorry for your loss*, or…*I know this is a difficult time for you*, or…*I'm here for you* (and *mean it*). We want to hear those cute and funny stories from their childhood and workplaces. These are things that we as survivors want to hear…it's music to us. It's comforting to hear these things coming from those who love and miss them too.

On the other hand, there are those who, although hopefully meaning well, just say the wrong things. The following is a list of what never to say or ask one who has just lost their spouse, life partner or loved one.

- He or she is in a better place.
- I understand.
- Don't feel bad.
- Don't cry.
- It's a blessing.
- God wanted him or her.
- It was his or her time.
- He or she is not suffering any more.
- You're young and pretty…you'll meet someone else.
- At least you have your children.
- Oh…you'll have another child.
- Are you going to sell your house? Worse yet…Do you *have* to sell your house?
- Now you can have things the way you want them.
- Are you feeling sorry for yourself?
- Last, but equally as important, do not **ever** tell the survivor to *"Get Over It"*.

Put yourself in the shoes of the survivor. Have you truly experienced this pain, this loss, to say you understand? Being there, being comforting, and listening to them is a gift.

And please…Don't ask specific details of the death. When the bereaved survivor is ready to say anything about the death, they will tell you. Please realize this is a very painful time in their life. It's traumatizing.

Your local hospice can give you handouts on ways to express your sympathy. Your library and bookstores will have books on the subject too. Kindnesses are rewarding.

8

"They may forget what you said, but they will never forget how you made them feel."
—*Carl W. Beuchner*

Additional Notes

and then there was one

Often it is the case when you lose someone dear to you, that reading a book, watching a movie, listening to tapes, or visiting websites, would be the last thing you think about.

However, after trudging through the first few months, the fog will start to lift and you will feel a need to research the subject of grief and get help—if for no other reason than to confirm your sanity, and get valid endorsements for your feelings.

This will be a good experience. We are all thrown into a world that we didn't choose, and know nothing about. It hurts, and it hurts deeply.

Your grief counselor, hospice personnel, librarian, or bookstore, will be able to recommend certain books, movies, tapes and websites that can present specifics geared towards your personal loss, and your emotional state at the time. Keep in mind there are books in Braille for the blind also.

Everyone's situation is different, and emotions and responses are as varied as any movie or book title. We are all different, and no one resolution works for everyone. But they do offer reinforcement of the fact that you are not alone in your grief. This should bring you some comfort during your journey.

A few movies I found comforting were:

- *Secondhand Lions*
- *Up*
- *My House in Umbria*

A documentary that was very moving and a 'must-see':

- *Consider the Conversation*

8

Lyrics to songs take on a whole new meaning.

Special Recognition

*T*his workbook could not have happened without the help from the following professionals who are respected members of their communities. I thank them many times over for their kindness, loving support and on-going contributions. Their integrity and passion for their profession shines through.

Leighton H. Rockafellow, Esq., Tucson, Arizona. A dear friend of mine for nearly 40 years. Thank you Leighton for always believing in me, for being in my corner, and for your support & contributions to the workbook; Dr. Timothy Munderloh, D.C., Munderloh Chiropractic, Flagstaff, Arizona. Unbridled concern for his patients; Norvel Owens, Norvel Owens Mortuary, Flagstaff, Arizona. A man who glows with compassion and caring for all; Andi Kleinman, Graphic Designer, Flagstaff, Arizona. Artistic genius. Thank you, Andi, for all the beautiful graphics, and time spent editing. You are a true, special friend; Martin E. Battock, Financial Planner, Mesa, Arizona. For your kindness and coming on board with such short notice; Deputy Joel Winchester, Coconino County Sheriff's Office for your insight on Identity Theft. Andre Morris, *my* PC Techs, Phoenix, Arizona. Thanks so much for all your help with the computer. You are a dear; William R. Whittington, Esq., Estate Planning Attorney, Prescott, Arizona. Thank you for sharing your intellect at our workshops. You are a wonderful person and truly appreciated. People love your entertaining presentations; Patti J. Shelton, Esq., Estate Planning Attorney (Retired), Shreveport, Louisiana. Our immediate bond and mutual desire to help people has really touched me. You are so kind and delightful...it shows at all of our workshops. People adore you. Thank you for being a friend; Kenneth J. Peace, Esq., Scottsdale, Arizona. Your wonderful presentations touch all who hear you. Eliza Daley-Read, Esq., Estate Planning Attorney, Flagstaff, Arizona. You have been so wonderful. Sincere appreciation.

Others who have come on board more recently...sincere gratitude for so lovingly giving of your time and intellect to make the workshops such a success. To name a few:

Jeffrey P. Hall, Esq., Estate Planning Attorney, Chandler, Arizona; James D. Schwartz, CFP®, CDFA™, Scottsdale, Arizona; Phoebe Harris, Esq., Estate Planning Attorney, Tucson, Arizona; Jeff Schenk, AAMS®, Phoenix, Arizona; Susan Robbins, Esq., Sun City, Arizona; Matthew Roberts, MBA, Phoenix, Arizona; Adam J. Potash, LPN. CHPLN, Oncology Physician Liaison, Hospice of the Valley, Phoenix, Arizona; Representatives from other Hospices throughout Arizona; and so many others to mention... Mr. Al Bell, Founding Member and Past President, California Planning Round Table, Peoria, Arizona; Major Jonathan Burgess, USMC, Yuma, Arizona; Gail Majors, Tempe, Arizona; And not to overlook another wonderful supporter in Wisconsin, Donna Hutter, who gives of her time to help others learn the importance of planning through workshops she arranges there in her state. Hats off to her and all those she recruits to speak for her, including Rainbow Hospice Care.

And to the Colleges and Learning Groups who invite us into their classroom...thank you for embracing our efforts and helping us reach your members.

I wish to thank all of our friends who rescued me when my husband died so unexpectedly. Few are blessed with people like those who surrounded me during this horrible time. They stayed with me, sheltered me, fed groups of people for an entire week, made all my business phone calls for months afterward, took care of my finances and funeral arrangements, and came rushing to my aid in every other way possible without my asking. Not only were they there during that first week, but remained (and continue), ready willing and able to be there for me if ever I need anything.

Marlene Dietrich once said…"the only friends that matter, are those you can call at four o'clock in the morning." The following qualify that statement…

My daughter, Marlies, and son Michael; granddaughter, Alex; my sisters, Dolores & Pearl, brother Steve, and our mother Louise. Our friends Tom, Tim & Denise Neal, Gary & Chris Barrett, Mike & Karen Chapman, Dean Miller, Teresa Gabriel Coyne, Baby Jill, Gene & Alison Hassler, Ralph & Kathy Homan, Bob & Jeannie Kimes, Tom & Mary Knight, Jim & Reneé Jones, Bob & Carol Greene, Patricia Poulin, Skip & Chris Heyer, Richard & Linda Fox, Brian & Christa Miller, Aaron Fox, Jean Benson, Carole, Lynda, and all others in our circle of friends and family too numerous to mention. Many thanks also to my new friends—Celia, (counselor extraordinaire), Sandy, Beverly and Janice—we share the same journey.

There are so many more people out there that have touched my life and helped me along the way—from those I've met in workshops, all who contribute to workshops, and everybody in between. I am more grateful than you could ever imagine.

A heartfelt "*Thank You*".

Charlotte

Life's most urgent question is: "What are you doing for others?"
—*Martin Luther King, Jr.*

Additional Notes

To My New Friends:

Doesn't it make you feel good to have this workbook completed? Your loved ones will appreciate this so much. You have done them a huge favor. Remember now, keep this in a safe place.

For me, this has truly been a labor of love, and very healing knowing that I am helping others avoid many unintended consequences. It is my hope to continue educating people regarding their end-of-life plans. To that end, and in order to continually grow and improve the function of this workbook, your comments, suggestions, and any contributions you can make to this project are very important and are very welcomed. Let me hear your story.

Feel free to visit my website at **www.therewasone.com** and visit the **'blog'** section. As I learn new information, I post it here to help you keep your workbook current.

Please drop a line with any ideas, thoughts, comments, or experiences you may have to more satisfy the needs of our new friends. My contact information is below.

With Sincere Appreciation, *Thank you*

Charlotte

e-mail:

Charlotte.fox@therewasone.com. Put *"workbook"* in subject line.

or mail to:

Charlotte Fox
P.O. Box 22333
Flagstaff, AZ 86002

8

...because time and unforeseen occurrence befall them all.
—Ecclesiastes 9:11

Additional Notes

and then there was one

*A*s I started to pen the final touches in this workbook, the morning news spoke of a young woman who had just given birth to a son—a son by her husband—a young man who was killed in Iraq that same morning.

My mind drifted to three friends, who, five weeks after my husband died, lost their husbands in the stormy seas off Rocky Point, Mexico. A fourth friend lost both her husband and their son in the same incident.

As difficult as it was to have my husband die while lying next to me in our bed, I can now count my blessings. At least I knew where he was and how he died. As unlikely as it was at the time, it is a comfort to me now that I got to hold him one last time, and kiss him goodbye. That poor young mother and my friends never had this opportunity.

In these difficult times that we now live, it is so important in life to learn to appreciate our *haves* and to not dwell on our have-nots.

As you heal, grab onto and embrace every moment of the rest of your life. Love like there is no tomorrow...because there may not be.

With Love and Hope,

Charlotte

8

Additional Thoughts for Your Loved Ones

Perhaps a written history to pass along? Have some cute stories?

and then there was one

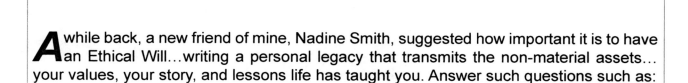

Awhile back, a new friend of mine, Nadine Smith, suggested how important it is to have an Ethical Will...writing a personal legacy that transmits the non-material assets... your values, your story, and lessons life has taught you. Answer such questions such as:

> ...What has given your life meaning?
> ...What has been the guiding principle of your life?
> ...What have you learned in all your years of living that you'd like your descendants to know?

Another idea to think about, is perhaps writing letters to your loved ones to be opened after you die. Being loving, forgiving and understanding will be music to them. Recall the fun things. This is a beautiful gift to hand down.

Additionally, as younger people, we had been so busy with working and raising our family that we often don't think to ask the older ones in our family about *their* life as children and growing up and raising their families. What they went through...their hardships... their good times. Don't hesitate to do this and ask the older generations about their lives. You can't even imagine the interesting stories they will have. I was fascinated by things I learned.

8

"What you have learned is as valuable as what you have earned."
—Susan Turnbull

Remarriage Checklist

There may come a time when you decide to remarry.
If so, please refer to this list

1. If you or your future spouse receives support, alimony, or Social Security payments, how will remarriage affect these payments?
2. How will income—that each party or both parties receive—be handled?
3. Is it better to file joint or separate income tax returns?
4. How will monthly expenses be paid? Split evenly? Paid from one account or another?
5. Does each spouse understand the debt, income, and asset situation of the other spouse?
6. Should a Prenuptial Agreement be considered?
7. How will estate planning documents be handled?
8. Should credit cards be obtained in single or joint names? Who is responsible for paying the debt accrued on these cards?
9. If one or both of you operate a personal business, what will happen to it should a divorce take place?
10. If each party has a home, which home will the couple live in and how will it be titled? What happens to the survivor spouse should the owner spouse pass away?
11. If an inheritance is expected, how will inherited assets be titled, managed, and maintained?
12. If a new car, boat, piece of land, or computer is purchased, how will this property be handled?
13. How will the assorted accounts be split should one spouse pass away?
14. If a divorce occurs, will spousal support (alimony) be paid, and by whom?
15. What are your obligations to your children and parents? What are your new spouse's obligations to his or hers?
16. If both parties have their own financial advisor (or other professional), which advisor will be consulted after the marriage?
17. Which holidays and vacations are spent with which families?

Provided by and reproduced with permission from
James Schwartz, CFP® CDFA™, RICP™, 8426 E. Shea Blvd., Scottsdale, AZ 85260

and then there was one

8

Instructions to spiral-bind or fit into a three-ring notebook

To have this workbook fit into a three-ring presentation binder, your printing facility or office supply store must first trim off the binding, then trim both the top and bottom a little to make the height 11", and punch holes to accommodate the binder. You can then slip the cover of the book (don't punch holes in cover) in the outside front and back of the binder.

To put a spiral bind in the workbook, they need to follow the above procedure prior to punching, and thread with the spiral bind instead. (Cover gets threaded also.)

Remember to check my "Blog" tab on my website for any
new information I may post there.

www.therewasone.com

While on the website, please click on the little
facebook icon 'f' and 'like' us on facebook. Thank you

*T*he initial shock of death of a loved one can be crippling and overwhelming. Giving my daughter a jump-start to the process will be helpful to everyone involved.

In my personal book, I wrote directions to my daughter so she would have a starting point after my death. 1) Call my friends for spiritual needs or arrangements; 2) Notify my selected body-donation entity; 3) Notify my life insurance company. I even tabbed some pages I felt were more relevant than others.

If you like this idea, use the space below, or a separate sheet of paper to slip right inside the front cover.

Kindest Regards,

Charlotte

CPSIA information can be obtained
at www.ICGtesting.com
Printed in the USA
LVOW09s0746060217
523238LV00001B/1/P